Eddie Paul's Paint & Bodywork Handbook

W9-AYO-466

©2006 Eddie Paul

Published by

krause publications
A subsidiary of F+W Media, Inc.

700 East State Street • Iola, WI 54990-0001
715-445-2214 • 888-457-2873
www.krausebooks.com

To order books or other products call toll-free 1-800-258-0929
or visit us online at www.krausebooks.com or www.Shop.Collect.com

Library of Congress Catalog Number: 2005935182

ISBN 13: 978-0-89689-233-0
ISBN 10: 0-89689-233-6

Designed by Jon Stein
Edited by Brian Earnest

Printed in China

Contents

Dedication

This book would not be possible without the support of my wife, Renee Paul. She and my daughter, Ariel, have both been so understanding of the long hours I've spent behind my computer and out in the shop. Renee has always been behind me and supported me in some of my most outrageous ideas and concepts and stopped me from doing the crazy stunts that could have possibly led to my early demise. For some reason, she seems to find much more peace of mind with me writing these books than blasting down the highway at 200 mph on one of my custom Boss Hoss V-8 motorcycles or bumping heads with an angry shiver of flesh-eating bull sharks to test the bite-resistance of one of the plastic shark suits that I designed. Thank you, Renee, for understanding and helping me as much as you do.

Thanks also to Brian Hatano for all the help on the books and the long hours of hammering, shaping, sanding and painting out in the shop to generate the subject matter that goes into these books. We don't just write books, we also perform the work that we write about, which means that we are often at the shop seven days a week for 16 hours a day building cars and bikes, maintaining equipment, rewiring the shop for new equipment, and learning how to use the new equipment. Most of the photos in this book show members of my crew performing the work on various cars in my shop. Most of my time is consumed with designing, meeting with customers, interviews, and working behind the camera to take the photos. If I *am* in front of the camera, then Brian is the one behind it getting me in the shot. Together, we write, photograph, weld, program, grind metal, paint and even clean up the shop. Then, when we have a vehicle to show, we hit the road, going from one car show to the other to display the creations that were built at Customs by Eddie Paul.

Foreword

By Brian Hatano

Good training always — I repeat, *always* — begins with fundamentals. Acquiring skills without having any lessons on the fundamental aspects of painting, dent repair, or anything for that matter, is a journey down a long and bumpy road, otherwise known as learning the hard way. To learn skills the hard way is not necessarily a bad thing, but when it comes to work on cars, it's a process that takes longer and usually requires a sacrificial vehicle or two to learn on. There are a few good ways to go about the learning process. Finding a knowledgeable and extremely patient journeyman to take you under his wing and oversee your education is one. Enrolling in a trade school is another. But for those of you who have a high level of adeptness with your hands and strong motivation to get started, then garnering all the information that you can from books like this will set you off in the right direction.

If you don't know Eddie Paul or are wondering exactly what qualifies him to write a book on the subject of automotive painting and bodywork, then allow me to introduce him. I hold the dubious honor of having worked with Eddie since 1979; a long, long stretch of time that we're both very proud of, but also hesitant to acknowledge to most people because it reveals our ever-escalating age. I took a 10-year hiatus from the rigors of customizing, building movie cars, fabricating and painting to venture off into the world of publishing, becoming the editor for magazines such as *Sport Compact Car, Car Craft* and *Drag Racing*. Little did I realize at the time that all of my creative editing skills would later come in handy again when I reunited with Eddie. It seems like just a few years ago that we were the new guys of customizing with plenty of raw talent, creativity and energy. We're as creative and energetic as ever, but our talents are now refined and spread out over numerous technologies. When I first got into automotive painting and bodywork, all I knew about either field was that I wanted to do it. I possessed a fair amount of mechanical engine-building experience, but as far as enhancing or repairing the aesthetic quality of a car goes, I was out of my area of expertise. Still, I jumped right into the deep end by asking for and getting a job at Customs By Eddie Paul. Back then, Eddie's shop was not much bigger than a three-car garage with an old spray booth around the back. We had no computers, car lifts or anything that was close to being state-of-the-art. Our equipment consisted of a couple of floor jacks, a beat-up old power post, a heavy-duty vise mounted on a steel truck wheel, a Victor gas torch, and a Tri-Arc MIG welder that would deliver a 220-

volt shock every once in a while when you least expected it. Our spray booth filter was one of those that used a roll of toilet paper for an element, and the compressor had to be drained twice a day. So it was by necessity that I learned to do everything the old-fashioned way — by hand. And Eddie was the man who taught me so much of what I know now about fabrication, problem solving, figuring things out and making things work. Eddie Paul is perhaps the only customizer today who has had a working rapport with legendary builders and painters such as Ed "Big Daddy" Roth, Gene Winfield, Dean Jeffries, and even the elusive Von Dutch. Even after all these years, I still consider it an honor to work side-by-side with Eddie on a project, and I continue to learn from him whenever I do. The amount of knowledge, not to mention the tales of the old days, inside Eddie's mind overload the capacity of the average brain. Today, Customs By Eddie Paul is part of E.P. Industries, Inc., a business that develops and prototypes new inventions and technologies such as lasers, pumps and engines; manufactures tools; films, edits and produces videos and animations; and we still manage to build a custom car or motorcycle every now and then. The shop is still located in El Segundo, California, but has expanded no less than five times since that first dusty garage next to the tow yard on Nevada Street. The business now thrives in a 25,000-square-foot facility that is outfitted with just about every piece of high-tech computerized machinery in existence. Although the shop, the equipment, and most of the people working for Eddie have evolved over time, the one thing that really hasn't changed much is how we approach a project. The simplest way is still usually the best way to do a job. That means utilizing those fundamental skills that we learned so long ago with nothing more than basic hand tools. And nobody that I know of is more qualified to explain the fundamentals of automotive painting and bodywork than the guy who showed them to me: Eddie Paul.

Introduction

AUTO BODY REPAIR AND PAINT REFINISHING ARE TWO VERY LUCRATIVE VOCATIONAL FIELDS IN THE AUTOMOTIVE INDUSTRY BECAUSE, LIKE ENGINE MECHANICS, THERE ARE SO MANY VARIABLES THAT TO BECOME PROFICNENT REQUIRES YEARS OF EXPERIENCE. THIS IS THE MAIN REASON WHY AN ESTIMATE TO REPAIR A SMALL DENT ON YOUR LATE-MODEL CAR OR TRUCK CAN EASILY REACH A $1,000! AND IT'S ESTIMATES LIKE THAT THAT MAKES IT QUITE APPEALING TO TRY TO DO IT ALL YOURSELF.

AS ANY GOOD-STANDING MEMBER OF THE DIY (DO-IT-YOURSELF) CLUB WILL ATTEST, PERFORMING ANY WORK OR MODIFICATION ON YOUR OWN CAR CAN BE EXTREMELY SATISFYING IF, AND ONLY IF, YOU KNOW WHAT YOU'RE DOING. EVEN VERY BASIC BODYWORK AND PAINT PROCEDURES FALL INTO THE CATEGORY OF ADVANCED DIY, REQUIRING A MUCH HIGHER LEVEL OF SKILL THAN, SAY, CHANGING YOUR OIL AND FILTER. THERE IS ALSO THE EXPENSE OF TOOLS AND MATERIALS TO CONSIDER, TOO, SO IT WOULD BE SAFE TO SAY THAT TRYING YOUR HAND AT ANYTHING OTHER THAT BASIC BODYWORK OR PAINTING WOULD BE AKIN TO JUMPING INTO THE DEEP END OF THE POOL.

COLLISION REPAIR, AS OPPOSED TO BASIC BODYWORK, INVOLVES ANY TYPE OF EXTENSIVE DAMAGE OF THE FRAME OR UNITIZED BODY THAT WOULD MAKE THE REPAIR IMPOSSIBLE TO PERFORM IN ONE'S GARAGE OR DRIVEWAY. MOST COLLISION REPAIRS ON LATE-MODEL VEHICLES TODAY ARE BEST DONE ON A COMPUTERIZED AND VERY EXPENSIVE FRAME MACHINE THAT ONLY A WELL-EQUIPPED BODY SHOP OR DEALERSHIP WOULD HAVE. THEREFORE, ALL PROCEDURES THAT WE WILL COVER IN THE BASIC PAINT AND BODYWORK HANDBOOK WILL BE BASIC ONES GEARED FOR THE FIRST-TIME BEGINNER, NOVICE, OR WEEKEND BODY MAN AND PAINTER; IN SHORT, EVERYONE IN THE DIY CLUB.

WHAT DIFFERENTIATES A PROFESSIONAL AUTOMOTIVE PAINTER OR BODY MAN FROM AN AMATEUR DO-IT-YOURSELFER? TWO THINGS: EXPERIENCE AND TOOLS. AS YOU STRIVE TO GAIN MORE EXPERIENCE AND TOOLS, IT WON'T TAKE LONG TO REALIZE THAT THE TWO GO HAND IN HAND. ONE WITHOUT THE OTHER IS ABSOLUTELY USELESS. FOR THIS REASON, I EMPHASIZE A BALANCE BETWEEN ACQUIRING TOOLS AND LEARNING THE TECHNIQUES AND TRICKS OF THE TRADE THAT I PLAN TO SHARE WITH YOU.

IF YOU BREAK DOWN THE INDIVIDUAL SKILLS AND TECHNIQUES INVOLVED WITH GOOD BASIC BODYWORK, YOU'LL FIND THAT THERE ARE MANY SIMILARITIES WITH THOSE OF CUSTOM METAL FABRICATION. I WOULD VENTURE TO SAY THAT A GOOD BODY MAN WITH JUST A LITTLE BIT OF CREATIVITY WILL MAKE AN EXCELLENT FABRICATOR.

THE SAME HOLDS TRUE WITH AUTOMOTIVE PAINTING. WHILE MOST PEOPLE MIGHT RELATE A "CUSTOM" PAINT JOB TO BRIGHT GRAPHICS, PEARLS AND CANDY COLORS, MY DEFINITION OF A CUSTOM PAINT JOB IS NOT SO MUCH IN THE COLOR AS IT IS IN THE PREPARATION — IMMACULATE, METICULOUS PREPARATION! ANY PAINTER WHO DEVELOPS THE SKILLS TO REFINISH A CAR WITH NEAR-PERFECT RESULTS IN A FACTORY COLOR IS CAPABLE OF DOING THE SAME WITH CUSTOM COLORS.

SO WHETHER YOUR GOAL IS TO BECOME A BODY MAN OR A FABRICATOR, A PAINTER OR A CUSTOM PAINTER, IT ALL BOILS DOWN TO LEARNING AND MASTERING THE BASICS.

Chapter One

Bodywork Basics

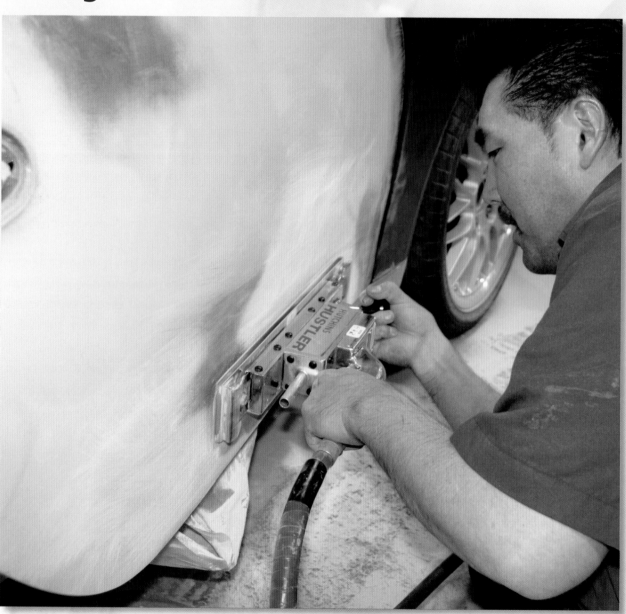

This is an example of why you should do the best job you can when you repair, customize or paint a car. This Italia once belonged to actor Lyle Waggoner, and we did the customizing on it for him. The car was recently brought to our shop more than 30 years after we worked on it and the quality has paid off — the car looks as good as the day we delivered it to Lyle.

Bodywork consists of all of the steps required to repair a damaged panel up to the paint prep stage. These steps include assessing the damage, grinding, repairing or reshaping the metal, molding and filling, and sanding the surface until it's smooth and even with the rest of the panel.

The Logic Behind Body Repair

Most automobile bodies are manufactured out of flat, annealed steel plates that are stamped into their final form using large 300- to 500-ton presses. As the metal is pressed into the final shape by its solid steel male and female dies, it undergoes a bit of work hardening that helps the metal maintain the refined shape that was intended for the conclusive product. The piece is then welded or bolted together with other stamped pieces to provide the entire automobile with a stronger overall shape. Every automotive body as a whole has enormous structural integrity as well as refinement of design and function. Each gentle curve and subtle body line gives the body as much added strength and rigidity as it does styling.

In a perfect world, the autobody repair and refinishing industries would not be needed. Cars would never break or rust out, drivers would never have accidents and paint would last forever. But the truth is that auto repair and refinishing are big businesses in which many people are able to make good livings. Autobody repair, customizing and painting skills are valuable commodities in the automotive workforce.

As I wrote this book we were running out into the shop to build a few cars for the animated show for PIXAR/Disney called, strangely enough, *CARS*. This is the Porsche named Sally, and even though it is going to be used for only about a year to advertise the movie, we planned to build it so it will last 100 years. After all, it is a Porsche, a short Porsche...with a really high roof... but nonetheless, a Porsche.

Bodywork and painting tools and materials have evolved over the years in an effort to streamline the various repair processes and make each step easier, faster and more efficient. Where once the most sophisticated tools of repair

After this '58 Corvette was hit in the front left fender, the driver had the insight to save all the pieces. The repair can be equated to assembling a jig-saw-puzzle, with resin. Without the parts, we would need to build and sculpt the missing area to build the fiberglass over this "plug," then remove the plug from below.

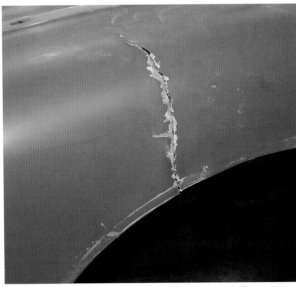

The same 'Vette showed a simple, but common, crack that was a result of a compression impact. This area can simply be cut along the crack with a saber saw, relieving the stress held in by the ends for the ragged break in the glass. Once the cut is made, the panel will align easily for repair. The crack will get a "V" groove ground in it and fiberglass matt and resin added as a repair agent.

consisted of a tape measure and a straightedge, shops now use computerized equipment with digital accuracy. The refinishing industry has also seen much change over the years. Still, in spite of the many changes, technology has not been able to eliminate the need for basic repair skills for fixing dents and spot painting panels. Much of the same tools and techniques that have been used for decades are still the best and only way to get a job done.

Anything from a wayward shopping cart or a careless swing of a car door in the grocery store parking lot, to a mild fender bender on your way to or from the store can result in a blemish to an otherwise perfect car. Depending on the severity and force of the impact, the metal could have just pushed inward slightly with only a small crease around the perimeter of the indentation. Mild damage such as this can occasionally be repaired with only some light hammer-and-dolly work, or sometimes with just a gentle push from the backside of the panel. Unfortunately, however, easy fixes are rare. Whenever the shape of metal is forcibly changed, the result is a modification of the metal's properties at and around the area where the reshaping, or damage, has occurred. If a damaged panel exhibits any sharp bends or creases where none existed before, it's a sure bet that the metal is stretched and cannot be pushed or tapped back into shape without getting into some refinishing work. But before we get into the process of repainting, there are several chapters worth of tricks, techniques and tools to

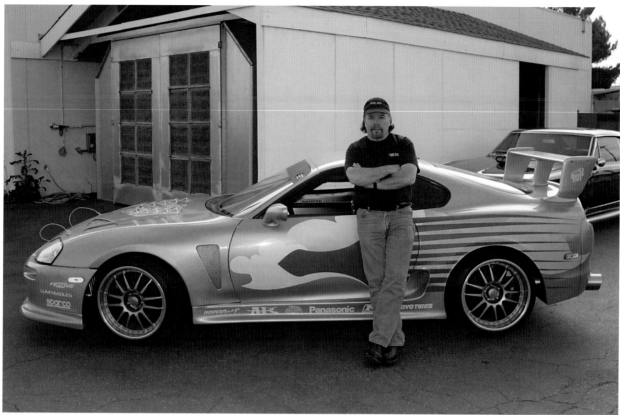

This is the Supra that performed the bridge jump in *2Fast 2Furious*. It looks as good as the first day it rolled in front of the cameras. Movie cars are a good example of fast body and paint repair as they are constantly being wrecked and repaired. Most of the time you only have a few days to repair a car that has been practically totaled.

cover as we discuss all of the things you'll need to know about the basics of auto body repair.

The need for basic bodywork, or as it is also commonly referred to, "dent repair," has been around ever since the first steel-bodied cars began to take the place of the horse and carriage. It's very likely that the art of metal restoration dates back even further than the automobile. For instance, I'm sure that any knight in shining armor surely would not have entered into battle with an unsightly indentation in his steel suit; so the village blacksmith or whomever was responsible for bumping ("bumping" is an antiquated term for straightening or hammering sheet metal back into original form) the metal back into shape could have very well have been the medieval precursor to the body man of today. Think of the metal armor that was effectively pounded into shape back when hand tools consisted of no more than a big hammer and an anvil. How did these craftsmen shape metal with such crude tools and no formal training? And how did they make repairs?

The point is that you will not need a lot of fancy equipment to repair a dent in a car. All dealership body shops and many independent ones have state-of-the-art computerized body repair equipment that requires comprehensive training and regular updates in order to use. A heavy collision repair specialist must be certified to use these types of systems, but the reality of basic body repair work is that nothing "high-tech" has replaced the knowledge and experience that a real metal man must have. Becoming a good body man is not about having a lot of fancy tools; it's about knowledge of how to work with metal, how to shrink it, stretch it, shape it and weld it; and most importantly, how to "read" a panel by feeling it with your hand.

Getting "The Feel" of Things

To sum things up in a few simple words, you can't fix what you can't feel! Therefore, the ability to *feel* the slightest irregularity on a vehicle's body is the most important acquired skill of basic body repair. I'm sure that everybody's individual sense of feel is different and some of you may not have as much sensitivity as others. But believe it or not, there is a technique to feeling a panel and, with a few tips, you, too, can get the feel of flat panels, contours and irregularities.

Feeling, or reading, a dent is a skill that one acquires through time and experience. If you can see a dent, chances are that you can also feel it. However, as a dent repair progresses, the visual element diminishes as the panel gets closer and closer to its original shape. The eye can be deceived by any number of things, so you must rely on feel.

This fender panel was easier to repair than to replace and is a good example of a choice made by a body man based on monetary considerations only. It is obvious that with this late model car the parts are readily available, but either the time or cost of the part swung the body man into repair mode.

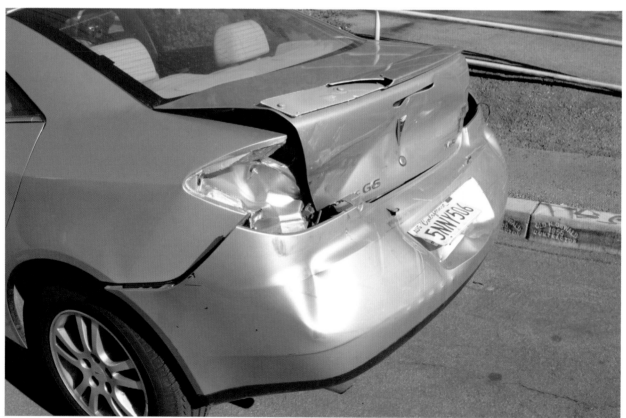

As bad as this looks, it is a fairly easy repair as most of the damage is to the trunk and bumper. A good body man can handle this in a few days. The rear body will require a pull as the car is fastened down and an old-style power post should do the trick quite well. The power post is a self-contained frame-pulling machine that is affordable to small shops.

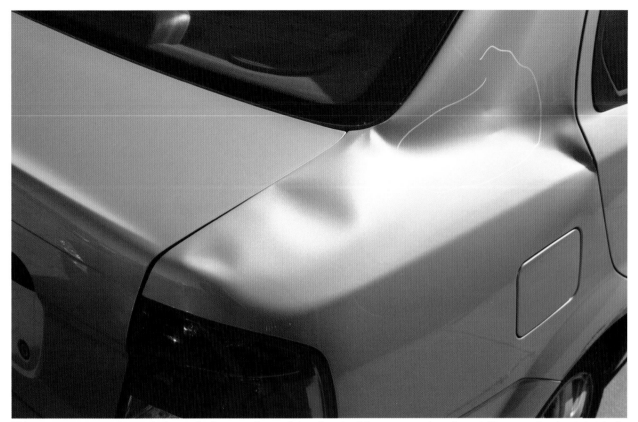

This rear upper quarter damage is the result of an out-of-control skate boarder. It is easy to repair as the metal has moved and not stretched. Much of it can be pushed out without much effort by starting from the outside edge of the damage and working toward the center.

The damage here was from a rear-end hit and was direct. The way to pull this dent out is by pulling directly rearward as you tap the high spots down.

This truck belongs to my animator Dave, and is a good case for a panel replacement, due in part to the extent of the rust and the mass availability of the parts. Better yet, Dave, replace the ugly truck with a new one!

This car demands the best of parts as well as repair, so don't try offshore parts or a fast, cheap repair.

The more creases the panel has, the stronger it is, and the easier it is to fix. Creases will help hold the shape in the panel. Try getting a flat panel flat again and you will see what I mean. And, you will learn a new word: "oil-canning."

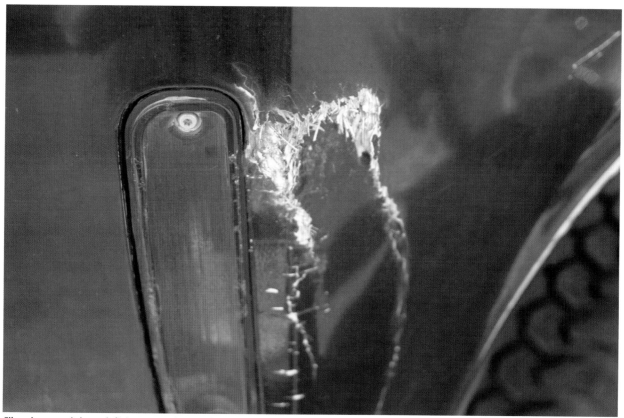

Fiberglass panels have definite pros and cons. They are good because they are a snap to repair. The bad side is the fibers can make your skin itch for a few days.

Fiberglass breaks easily, so all you have to do is put it back in position and re-glass the seams, add the correct filler, such as Tiger Hair, sand it down and you are done. There is no stretching or shrinking of metal involved.

This '65 Chevy shows the result of time well spent on block sanding a panel. Any waves or misaligned panels would show and not be correctable after the paint is applied, so spend the time to make sure the car is perfect before you paint it.

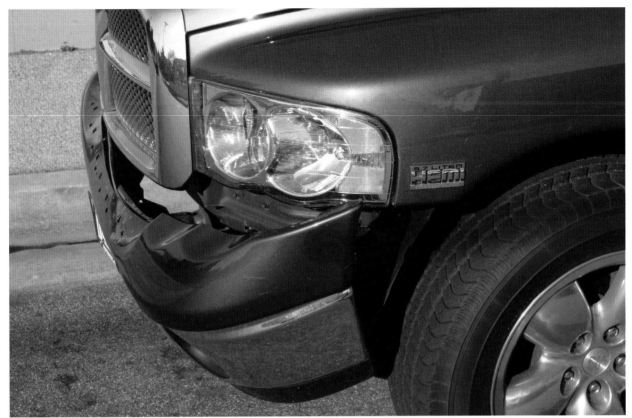

It is rare that damage is as isolated as this. On this repair a new bumper and a few hours of tapping will bring this back to new condition over a weekend.

Investigate The Damage

How was it hit? From what direction? How great was the force of impact?

These are some of the questions that a good bodyman must be able to find the answers to. Not unlike a crime scene investigation, this involves taking a close look at the damaged panel and trying to figure out how it happened. There are a lot of fascinating police dramas on television that take you into the world of forensics. Well, analyzing a dent to determine how to repair it requires a bit of autobody forensics as well. A good body man must always perform this step of diagnosis before blindly jumping in with the hammer and dolly. Although I specialize in custom work on cars and motorcycles, I have also been doing body repair work for as long as I can remember. Over the past three decades or so, I've gone through hundreds of employees, so I have seen the gamut of bodymen, from the "best" that can fix a dent without using any fillers to the ones that can turn a minor dent repair into a disaster by overworking the area and stretching the metal into a useless piece of scrap. Guys who start pulling and hammering before carefully analyzing the problem are the ones who rely heavily on plastic filler to fix their mess.

I used to have what I call a "flight of the imagination" theory that if you could tell exactly how a car was hit, and could reverse the damage in the exact opposite direction with the same force that made the damage in the first place, you could, with one pull, take the dent out of the he paint

You Can't Fix What You Can't Feel!

It is all but impossible to teach someone how to feel a dent or the high and low spots that might be present, or the ones that develop when body filler is used, without taking him or her through a physical demonstration. It helps to have a kind of hand-mind coordination to begin with, and assuming that you do, then there a few pointers that might help you get the feel of the situation.

First of all, most dents are not that hard to read. Most people, even a lot of body repairmen, tend to put their hand on the panel and slide it back and forth over the damage. Anybody can do this and feel the dent if it's large enough. But after the dent has been pulled and the area has been filled and sanded, things get a lot trickier. A subtle high or low spot or a combination of both can sometimes drive your hand and your mind to the brink of insanity as you repeatedly fill and block sand only to feel the same imperfections over and over. Depending on exactly where a low spot is on a particular panel, you could very easily be deceived into thinking you feel a high or low spot.

The first step of learning how to feel a panel is how to position your hand and what direction to move it in. Refer to the accompanying photos in this sidebar and read the captions for basic tips on how to feel, how not to feel, and how to see what you're feeling.

Brian was restoring one of the 1950 Mercs used in the movie *Cobra* that we had originally built for the film when he stumbled on a bad area in the body. We follow a step-by-step process for this type of repair.

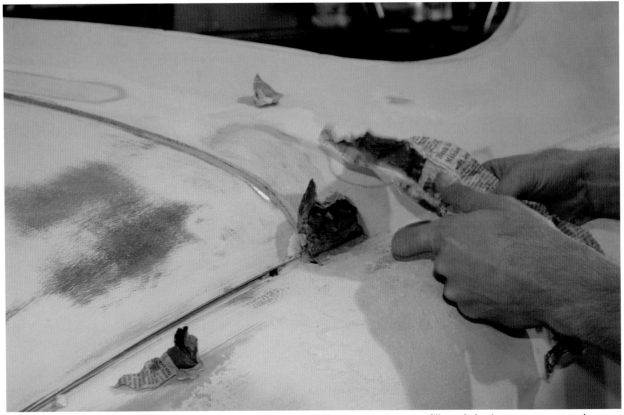

The first step was to pull out all the newspaper that was added by some "amateur" body man as filler to help give some support to the Bondo that was used to hide the rust hole. This is a perfect example of how not to fix a rusted area.

This little pocket contained a whole page of a San Diego newspaper, letting us know where and when the repair was done.

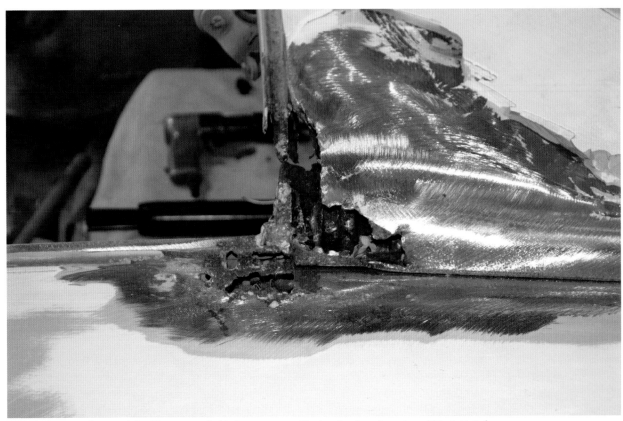

With the paper and some of the filler removed, the damage was evident and a plan of repair could be initiated.

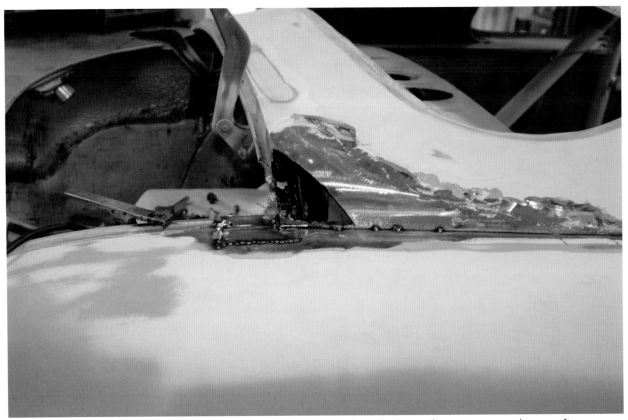

Cutting a few small pieces of metal and MIG welding them in place only took about 10 minutes. The area was as good as new after a very thin coat of filler was applied.

car. In theory, this would work, but in practice, it does not because most bodymen are much too quick to start beating a dent out without first reading the dent to see exactly how it happened.

Was it a direct hit perpendicular to the cars axis, or was it a glancing blow or even a combination of a direct hit that glanced off of the panel? Any principle damage to a car causes collateral damage to a car. For example, if the rear fender is hit, it will affect the door gap, trunk gap and a lot of the body alignment. It can cause unseen damage to the frame or even to the suspension and drive train. A small dent can have great underlying damage potential, so don't just look at the dent and think small. Look around and see what else might be affected by the impact. Force is the power or energy that the car was subjected to that caused the dent. You can figure that it'll take roughly the same amount of force to pull the dent out of the car that it took to make it. This may sound simple, but keep in mind that there are numerous factors to take into consideration. In other words, you can't just slam the backside of a dented fender and expect to fix it.

It's safe to say that no two dents are identical. For this reason, it's virtually impossible to categorize dents. Therefore, a bodyman must be prepared to deal with something new and unexpected when it comes to repair work. Learning the basics of bodywork is not a process that is ever really complete. But what you *can* learn here is that the key to fixing a dent is being able to analyze the damage and figure out how best to reverse the process.

Was it Hit Straight on, or From an Angle?

If a victim was mysteriously shot by a gun, one of the elements of solving the crime would be to determine the angle of trajectory. The same holds true when the victim is a smashed car. The bodyman can only start the repair properly if he knows from what direction the car was hit. "Now how the heck would I know this?" you ask. "I didn't see the accident!" Let me explain how to use a bit of "impression forensics" to help you read. or "reverse-engineer," the damage. Damage assessment is usually a simple matter of applying some common-sense and logic.

If the dent is somewhat symmetrical without a scrape mark on the painted surface, all indications point to an impact from a straight perpendicular hit. If, on the other hand, the paint is scraped and the dent is non-symmetrical or pushed up on one side, the dent was obviously caused by an indirect hit, and by looking at the direction of the paint scratches as well as the shape of the dent, you can assume that the impact came from one side or the other. To be more specific, if a panel is hit from a direction other than straight on, the affected metal will be left with somewhat of a wave-like impression. The metal was pushed *ahead* of the impact area. If the dent is new, you can also look at the scraped paint and see which way it hit because the paint will curl up on the end of the direction of the impact.

When I first got into body repair, my unadulterated curiosity for anything related to fixing a dent had me going to the local wrecking yard to study a variety of totaled-

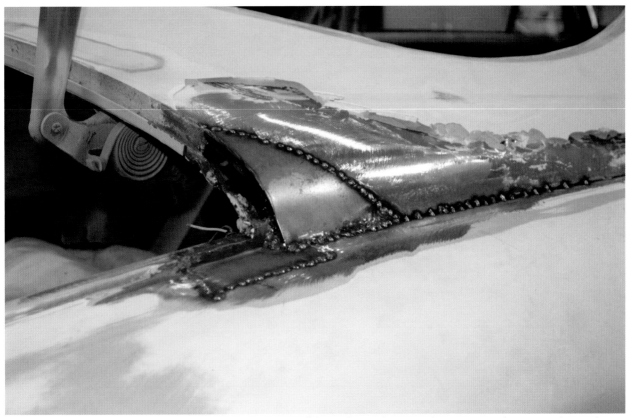

We matched the gauge of the original car body with small patches. If the patches are in an area that may rust again, we sometimes make them out of a thicker piece of metal.

out cars just to see if I could figure out how the accident occurred. The reason that this is so important (figuring it out, not going to wrecking yards!) is that it will help you figure out the direction that the panel must be worked as well as where to look for hidden damage. For example, if a car suffered a rear end hit and the gap between the door and front fender is closed up, that tells you there's much more damage than a smashed rear. Did you know that if a car is hit hard from behind, you could tell if the driver had the brakes on at the time of impact even if the car was towed from the scene of the accident (where you could have just looked for skid marks)? The clue can be found in the taillight bulbs. The bulb filaments get soft and weak when the light is on and a sudden impact is oftentimes enough to break the filament. So by seeing which bulb is out, a sharp repairman can tell if the brakes or headlights were on. This doesn't necessarily relate to body repair, but it proves that looking closely at certain parts of a car can tell you what it's been through.

If you look closely, a hit on a panel will very likely cause a series of deep ridges in the metal that radiate out from the point of impact. The ridge, or crease, that is furthest away from the main point of impact is where to begin the basic body repair. A smooth undamaged sheet of metal tends to be flexible to a degree. However, once an indentation is made into that sheet, the panel becomes more rigid. A dented fender or door panel exhibits the same characteristics. Therefore, once you begin to work the

creases out, the damaged panel will gradually become easier to work with. These radiant creases are actually holding the dent in. As long as you remember to work the damage from the outermost point towards the center of the impact, the metal will be much easier to hammer and dolly back into its original form.

The objective as you begin to hammer and dolly the metal is, at first, to relieve the stress of the creases and indentations. The initial body working is strictly rough-shaping until the metal is free of any sharp indentations. The goal is to work the panel back into shape without stretching the metal unnecessarily. Hammering directly at the center of the dent will cause the most stretching and make it almost impossible to return the metal back to original form. In most cases, there will be a small degree of stretch to contend with, but we'll get into that later.

The process of body repair and painting consists of individual steps that take you progressively closer to a finished job. The number of steps and the actual techniques involved will, of course, vary from car to car. When you begin your repair, you'll have to make the final call regarding which steps are needed and which are not. The following is a general outline of basic dent repair steps to use as a guide.

Damage Assessment: Feel the panel. Note the exact shape of the dent, check for high spots, low spots, and any collateral damage. Until you become totally familiar with this step, you can identify specific points of the damage

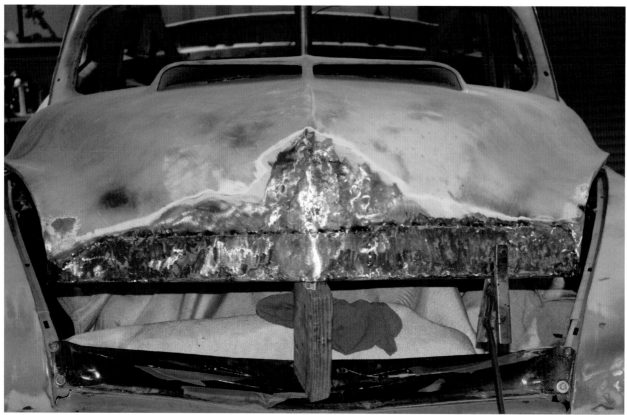

As is common on 1950 Mercs, the front of the hood of this movie car was heavily rusted. It was also damaged from all the stunts that the Merc had to go through in the filming of *Cobra*, so new metal was shaped and welded in place.

using masking tape and a marker. Tag the center point of the dent, the direction (if any) that the panel was hit, and the outer perimeter of the damage where you plan to start working the metal.

➤ **Access the Damaged Panel:** Remove inner panel, trim pieces, molding wherever they might interfere with your work. Save all parts and hardware for reassembly when the job is complete.

➤ **Tool Check:** Look into your tool box to make sure you have all the tools required for the job (see Chapter 2 on tools).

➤ **Rough It In:** Roughing a panel back into shape can involve anything from simple hammer-and-dolly work to attaching studs or drilling holes for slide pullers, to locating clamp points for making pulls with a hydraulic post puller or "dozer." Extensive damage requiring anything more falls into the heavy collision repair category.

➤ **Fine-tune the Metal Work:** More hammer-and-dolly work to bring down the high spots and bring up the lows. This step requires a lot of finesse with the hammer to avoid overworking the metal. Gentle hits are all that's needed. Hold the handle of the hammer at the midpoint or up high on the handle near the head to increase control.

➤ **Prep for Filling:** Prepping for body filler requires paint removal using a course-grit paper (36-grit) to expose bare metal. A high-speed sander/grinder can be used but the best paint removal tool is an orbital sander such as the Hutchins Model 2001 or a dual-action (DA) sander like

Hutchins' Model 3560. Filler should not be applied to anything other than clean, shiny bare metal.

➤ **Featheredge:** A good bodyman always feathers all paint edges before applying filler. The hard paint edge left from grinding must be tapered to a smooth, layered edge. This can best be accomplished with 120- or 150-grit sandpaper by hand or with the dual-action sander. A hard paint edge can get overlooked during the filler and primer applications and will show through after the paint cures.

➤ **Applying Body Filler:** The panel is ready for filling and molding as long as no high spots remain. A good-quality plastic filler such as Evercoat's Rage Extreme will fill minor low spots, grind marks and any other imperfections in the metal. Do not overlap filler onto the featheredged paint.

➤ **Work the Filler:** The process of smoothing the plastic filler begins with rough-shaping using a "cheesegrater" file. After grating, a sanding block mounted with 36-grit paper is used to level the filler. For large panel areas, a pneumatic air file such as the Hutchins Hustler Model 2000, 2011 or 2023 can be big time-savers. Follow up with block-sanding with 80-grit paper and the once-damaged area is ready for the first application of primer.

➤ **Paint Prep or Perfection:** At this point, the job can be handed off to the painter to begin the process of preparation for paint. Some body repairmen strive for perfection by taking the block-sanding stage one step further with 180-grit paper. This is a good thing!

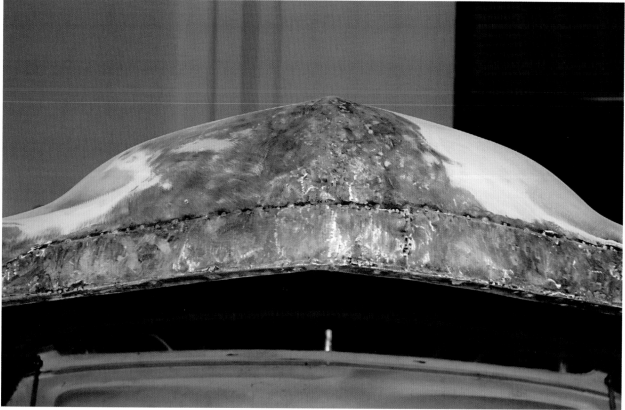

This replacement area was worked with hammer and dollies until it was in the original shape of the stock hood. We kept the hood on the car while we were working on it so we could constantly check it for fit with the contiguous panels.

Roughing It In

Most body damage will require some type of pushing or pulling device that can exert a force close to what was exerted the caused the damage in the first place. This equipment can range from a basic slide hammer to large hydraulic equipment. In the middle-range of such body tools is a portable power jack, otherwise known as a Porto-Power. This tool can perform many of tasks, but its primary talent is undoing the main force that caused the damage. It must be applied in the opposite direction of the damaging impact. Porto-Powers have become very affordable over the last few years. I remember the first set that I bought cost so much I had to make payments on it! Now you can get a fairly good-quality unit for a little over $100. Many of them come with a set of extensions and ends made to access those hard-to-reach areas. For a bit more money, you can get a "push-pull" system that will allow you to pull with the same tool.

Grinding the paint down to bare metal without heating it up is an art in and of itself. Grinding is a method of using a coated abrasive disk on a high-speed sander/grinder to tear the paint away from the metal. The disks utilize very small irregular abrasive particles glued to a disk in a gouging scraping motion called grinding. This method is fast, very effective and removes the paint in short order. However, the evil by-product of such friction is heat, and too much heat will cause the metal to expand and distort. This distortion is mostly temporary but partially permanent; the metal expands to a point when heated and contracts most

of the way when it returns to normal temperature. Notice that I said "most of the way." The problem is, once heated and cooled, metal will still remain a little bit larger than it started out. That's why when a car catches fire, all the panels buckle out of shape.

Reshaping the Metal

As you work the dent, you will find the areas that need work getting smaller and smaller. The tool selection must coincide with the progress of the work. No more heavy hammers or dollies are going to be needed if you did the job correctly. Depending on the quality of the roughing job you did, you could be down to very light well-placed taps instead of hard generally placed hits, so a set of finishing hammers with polished heads as well as a slapping spoon would be handy as well.

Once you notice the high and low spots begin to level out, you can either start filling the lows spots with a good-quality filler, or continue working the metal until little or no filler is required.

How do you get a feel for a low spot and what do you do about high spots? Well, this is where the "art" of bodywork comes in and "the feel" in effect becomes your guide, whereas the spraying on of a guide coat will give you a visual indicator of high and low spots by showing you where the sander went through the filler (showing the high spots) and where the sander did not touch the black guide coat (showing you the low spots).

On this famous car we needed to save the severely rusted-out hood, as it was the custom one we built for the film *Cobra*. The metal was replaced and hammered into shape and then worked to a finish with a thin coat of filler.

Within a few days the body is looking as it did when we first built the car. Notice the car is raised up to a comfortable working height using a Bend Pak scissor lift. This way we can lift or lower the car for working on different parts without having to sit on cold concrete.

This is the end result of the hood repair just before the car was delivered to the new owner. Any shortcut would have shown up here. Take your time and do the job right and you will not have to redo it later.

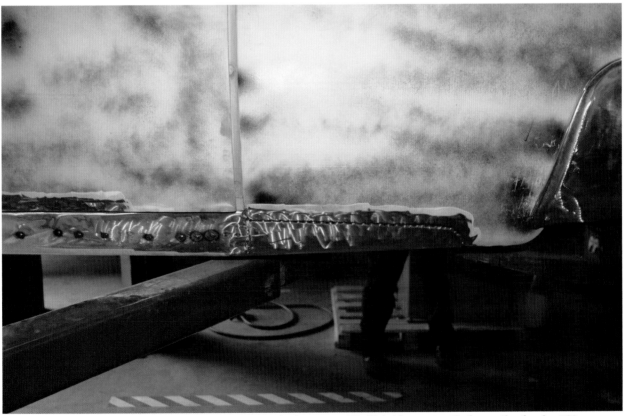

This is another patch panel we made for the same car as a result of more rust. We think this car sat out in the weather for about 20 years after it was wrecked during filming.

Without the tinning butter the lead would not stick to the metal. It is applied with the little acid brush.

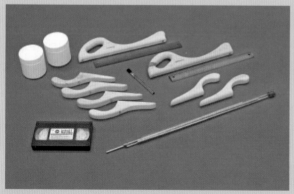

Here is a basic kit for performing lead filling. It is supplied by Eastwood and includes a how-to video, paddles, vixen files (one flat, one curved) tinning butter and a brush, as well as lead-free or leaded solder. Not shown is the tin of tallow or wax for waxing your paddles before you use them.

Why Lead?

The term "lead sled" generally refers to the old customs of the 1940s and '50s that, back in the day, often had a lot of lead slathered on them during the customizing process. In today's world of political correctness, health consciousness and "excessive safety for all," lead is looked upon as a health hazard and something everyone, including car restorers and customizers, should avoid. Too much exposure to it can lead to lead poisoning, known as "plumbism."

Lead can still be found all around us; it's in the solder that holds copper pipes together; in dirt, dust, toys (before 1976, dishes and mugs), old house paint (before 1987), bullets and shot, fishing sinkers, curtain weights, drinking water and pewter, which can contain as much as 4 percent lead.

Some of the symptoms of lead poisoning are: reduced IQ, slowed body growth, hearing problems, behavior or attention problems, failure at school, and kidney damage.

So how did so many early customizes live long and happy lives after adding thousands of pounds of lead to the many cars they have built over the years? Maybe they're just tough, I don't know.

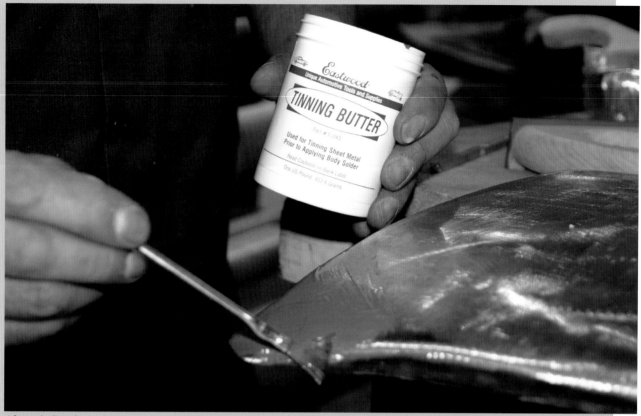

After grinding down the area to be repaired, the next step is to brush tinning butter onto the surface of the repair.

Anyway, most of the "lead" sold for leading is not lead at all anymore, but a new mixture of tin, copper and zinc. These new non-lead solders are now considered "safe" for application, consumption, injection, inhalation or exposure to almost any part of your anatomy.

So put away all the fear of being killed by your materials and "lead your sled" for the fun and education of it. It is easy and fast and will put you a notch higher as you gain the respect of your peers when they find out you can lead.

The process is simple and requires little in the way of equipment and tools. The skill required is not all that hard to gain, either. Kits like that offered by Eastwood go for about $100. This kit comes complete with: a flat paddle, a half round paddle, a file holder, English body file (flat) also known as a Vixen file, 1 lb. tin of tallow, 1 lb. tinning butter, five acid brushes, eight sticks of 70/30 body solder (70 percent lead and 30 percent tin) or lead-free solder and a video (#28023). And if you are using the real lead solder, remember not to ever sand it during the shaping and prep stages. **Lead should only be shaped with a file.** If you sand it you will produce lead powder, which can be dangerous to your lungs. So just file it so the byproduct is larger chunks of lead instead of fine

I like to wax up my paddles by first heating the wax with a small propane torch, then rubbing the paddles on the surface of the wax. This keeps the lead form sticking to the wood paddles.

Bodywork Basics

After adding tinning butter, simply apply heat to the work area with a small torch until the butter starts to get a bit shiny, showing that it is melting and sticking to the metal.

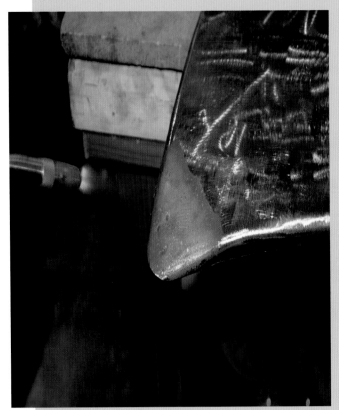

It will not take a lot of heat to melt the tinning butter, but the difference in appearance will be obvious. After that you are now ready to apply the solder.

particles. Many of the body solders can be applied using a propane torch.

To begin, locate the area that to be leaded in and make sure that the surface is ground down to the bare metal. Start by tinning the surface to be leaded. Without the tinning butter the lead will not stick to the metal. The butter can be applied with the little acid brush just before the surface is heated.

I like to wax up my paddles before I start leading by first heating the wax with a small propane torch, then rub the paddles on the surface of the wax. This keeps the lead from sticking to the wood paddles. The paddles will need frequent waxing as you proceed with the leading. If the lead starts sticking to the wood paddle, it's time to apply more wax.

Add heat from the propane torch to the work area until the area starts to get shiny. When the area becomes shiny, it means the tinning butter is melting and sticking to the metal. Tinning butter is a lot like a primer for lead — it helps it stick to the base metal. This will not take a lot of heat, but the difference in appearance will be obvious when it happens. At this point you are ready to apply the solder.

Pre-heat the solder bar with the torch to soften

Eddie Paul's Paint & Bodywork Handbook

Pre-heat the solder bar a bit to soften up the tip before you add it to the area you will be repairing.

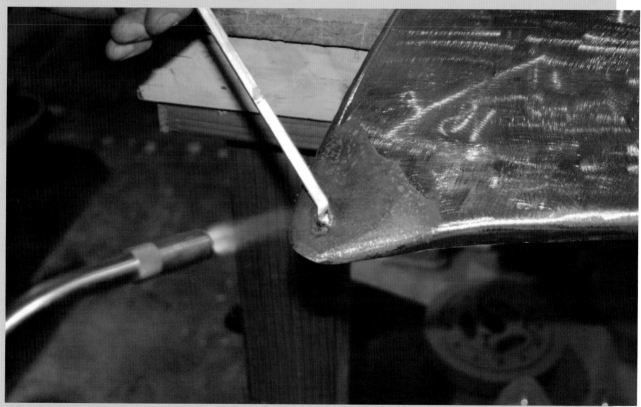

Once the solder is heated up a bit, you can apply it to the repair area and add more heat as you push the bar into the metal. It should push softly as it applies solder. Do not add too much or too little solder, just enough to fill the area. You can easily add more solder if needed. Try adding a bit less than you need at first, and as you learn what you are doing you will be able to judge how much you need for any given job.

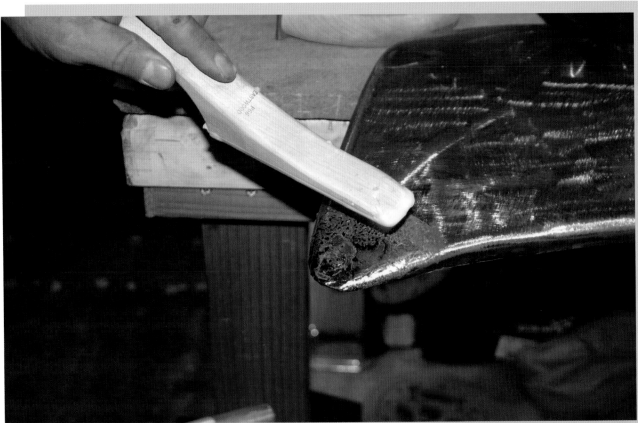

After you apply the solder, work it into shape by adding heat to the area occasionally and working it with the paddle.

up the tip of the solder before you add it to the area you will be repairing. Once the solder is heated up, you can apply it to the repair area and add more heat as you push the bar into the metal. It should push softly as it applies solder to the damaged area. Do not add too much solder, just enough to fill the area. You can easily add more solder if needed, so go easy at first and as you learn what you are doing. After you apply the solder you can work it into shape with a just by adding occasional heat to the area and working it with the paddle.

Once the solder is cooled it hardens and can then be easily shaped with a vixen file. If you find a low spot, simply add more solder. If the area is high, simply file it down more. You can add a small skim coat of spot putty or just add a bit more lead to fill the small imperfections before you prime the area.

Why lead instead of body filler? The main reason is that lead sticks better and is quite a bit stronger than body filler (the tensile strength is 6140 psi.). That's why automakers use it to bond and seal the seams of cars after spot-welding parts together.

The solder hardens as it cools, and can then be easily shaped with a vixen file. If you find a low spot, add more solder. If the area is high, simply file it down a little more.

This is the repair after filing and sanding. At this point you can add a skim coat of filler, or just add a bit more lead to fill the small imperfections. Then you are ready to prime the area.

We often take a car off the frame for high-end paint jobs. This 1966 LeMans was the foundation for a conversion into a 1967 *xXx* GTO. We set the body on a large dolly with casters so it could be moved around to different parts of our shop.

Once the under side of the body was painted and the frame restoration complete, we re-mounted the body back on the frame and got the car running. It's best to do all your heavy mechanical work before painting, or you'll risk ruining your new paint job.

Many times we use portable lifts to bring the car up to a better working height. This is one of the 1967 GTOs that we built for *xXx*. Under the shiny paint we found a ton of poorly prepared bodywork we needed to re-do. Even though it was only a movie car, we often over-do the body to make sure that body filler does not pop out during a stunt.

You should learn to get the feel for high and low without having to look at the area — that is unless you are the one in a million that can see the high and low spots without feeling them. This is very possible with a surface that is painted and glossy or even wet, but as soon as the surface is sanded or multicolored it will be all but impossible to see the high and low spots.

My shop manager, Brian Hatano, has a method of showing his helpers how he can feel the high and low spots. He will have them guide coat an area and then rub his hand across the surface and tell them where the high and low spots will appear without looking. Then he has them block sand the area and, sure enough, the metal shows where he said it will be high and the black paint stays where he said it will be low.

This leads me to an idea that you might try…I can't help it, it's the inventor in me! When you are block sanding an area, try marking what you think will be a low spot with a spray can of black guide coat and do not spray the areas that you think will be high spots. After sanding, see what the results are. If the paint remains untouched, then you have the feel. If not, keep practicing because a custom fabricator or bodyman without the feel is like a blind guide on a mountain climb. You have to be able to feel the metal to know what to do next or you will be working in the dark. You can train your hand just as you do with many things. This just takes a bit of dedication and time. Practicing can save you a lot of aggravation down the road.

When Is It Time For Primer?

This is really a loaded question; the work is ready for a coat of primer when it is straight and smooth and no sooner. Many bodymen are too anxious to prime a job and will sometimes bury a dent, either intentionally or unintentionally, with a heavy coat of primer thinking it will fill in the imperfections and that all will be good when the paint goes on. A good painter will catch this potential

The best way to remove the old body filler on this car was with an air hammer and Ajax chisel, We did this by getting the blade under the filler and on top of the sheet metal and forcing it off the car with the air hammer.

There are a number of ways to lift a low spot in a metal fender or panel such as this. We use this method if the underside of the panel is inaccessible and time is short. This process involves drilling a few holes and using them to pull a dent out.

Using a Morgan Nokker or slide hammer, simply put the "screw end" into one of the holes. Slide the weight back to the stop and kinetic energy will do the rest. Take a few light pulls, instead of one large one, or you will be tapping that area back down again.

Another good way to bring a low spot out and an adjacent high spot in, is to leave the slide hammer in place and while pulling out on it, tap the adjacent high spot down. This is somewhat like the hammer-off-dolly technique.

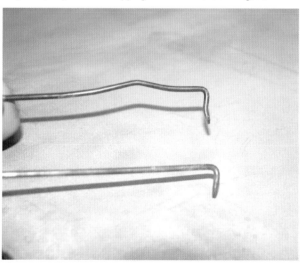

These are pull rods which are little more than bent rods that have been hardened to retain the shape. You can insert them into pre-drilled holes and pull up while tapping down on the closest high spot, just as we showed with the slide hammer. Remember that even though it may not seem like you are making progress, each and every blow of the hammer is moving metal, so be patient and work thoughtfully, not quickly.

This area is now within 1/8 inch of perfect and ready for the next step. If it were a show car we would metal finish it to perfection but that last 1/8 inch takes longer than the whole roughing process. The closer you try to get to perfect, the longer it takes. You may find that unless you are working on a classic or a show car, this may be "good enough" for you.

These studs can be grabbed by a special slide hammer that comes with the spot welder kit, and is used for pulling on the studs until the surface is flush. Then the studs can simply be twisted off. They are not reusable, we have tried, but they are cheap, so buy extras.

for problems, but if he doesn't, these "buried mistakes" will definitely come back to haunt both bodyman and painter as the thick primer shrinks.

There are no shortcuts and you should not rush to apply primer to the body unless it is absolutely ready to prime. When mixing and applying primer, always read and follow the manufacturer's recommendations for reduction, spraying tips and drying times. You can also choose a good-quality aerosol primer such as those offered by Evercoat. We use Evercoat products on a regular basis in my shop with excellent results. If the area to prime is large, you'll most likely be better off using a spray gun. I'll go more into gun selection later in the paint chapters, but for now, let me just say that a good-quality gun designed for primer application is recommended. I tend to favor the Devilbiss

Another method, instead of drilling a lot of holes, is to use a hand-held stud welder and weld little copper posts to the surface of the metal in the low areas.

line of guns, however, there are other manufacturers such as Sata and Sharpe that will do the job with professional results. Remember, primer is *not* liquid filler! It is an undercoat that promotes adhesion and provides a uniform base to paint over.

Primers and primer-surfacers are designed to fill very small surface irregularities and also to help protect any exposed bare metal from oxidizing when it is in contact with the oxygen in the air. Another function is to provide a substrate (paintable surface) with one uniform color to facilitate topcoat coverage. Most undercoats are available in black, light gray, dark gray, red, and white, and some can be tinted to match the color of the topcoat. Selecting an undercoat color that is close in shade to the topcoat is recommended for ease of coverage and accuracy of color match.

An important function of a primer undercoat is to provide maximum adhesion to the bare metal and properly sanded painted surfaces; the build quality allows enough thickness for block sanding. If you look into the various companies that manufacture automotive undercoatings, you'll find a mind-boggling array of special formulations that offer specific features such as high build, easy sanding, clog-free, corrosion resistance, flexibility and more. Unless you know what you want and need, you could easily be overwhelmed. I'm sure there are some people who miss the days of all-purpose acrylic lacquer primer that worked well for just about every job. In spite of all of the special undercoatings on the market, I still try to keep things as simple as possible in my shop by using one manufacturer — Evercoat — for all fillers and undercoats. Every paint manufacturer recommends that you stick with their system of chemicals from the primer on up. This is, of course, the surest and safest way to avoid any compatibility issues when it comes time to apply paint. For those who aren't familiar with the compatibility of different primers and paints, I highly recommend that you use the paint manufacturer's recommended undercoat until you become

A Vixen file is a special file that is designed for cutting lead and steel and can be used to cut the sharp edges of the fender down with ease. Eastwood sells these as well, in both flat and round styles.

A very important step that many people forget is to countersink all the holes. Filler can pop out when the fender flexes and counter sinking the holes keeps the filler from pushing inward. The residual filler that squeezes through the hole in the backside keeps the filler from popping outward. The countersink also gives more surface area for the filler to stick to.

more experienced.

Another type of primer that we use is called **etching** primer (also called acid-etch primer). As its name implies, etching primer chemically bonds, or etches, into the bare metal with the added ingredient of phosphoric acid. This special primer is used where corrosion problems exist, or when working with metals such as aluminum. Etching primer is not compatible with some sealers, primers and topcoats, so be sure to investigate compatible products before using it. Epoxy primers, or two-part catalyzed primers, cure through a chemical reaction, as opposed to solvent evaporation, when exposed to air. A catalyzed primer forms a good barrier coat between chemically unstable substrates and the topcoat. Other benefits include less shrinkage and excellent rust-inhibiting qualities.

Electrostatic primers are what most of the factories use.

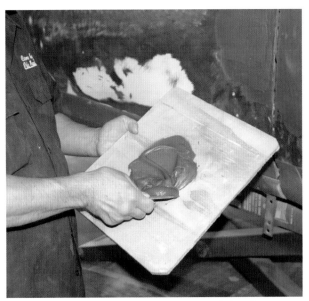

Many people apply too much filler, which not only will waste your filler, it takes more time to sand down. Try to get in the habit of just putting on as much as you need. Here, Brian uses a piece of plywood for his "mixing board" and cleans it after each use, keeping it in perfect condition.

A large DA sander is then used to sand the surface down; or you can pre-cut it, using a sure-form rasp, or cheese grater. This will show you the high spots that are in the fender.

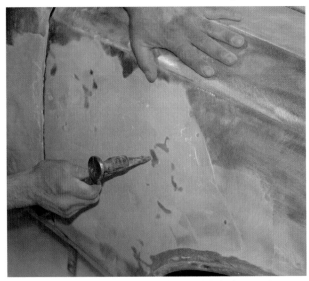

High spots can be picked down carefully with light hammering. Another thin coating of filler will be required.

The sure-form makes quick work of the excess filler on this fender, but you will need to rasp it at just the right time. If you wait too long the filler will be too hard and will have to be sanded. If you rasp it too soon, you will probably need a new rasp.

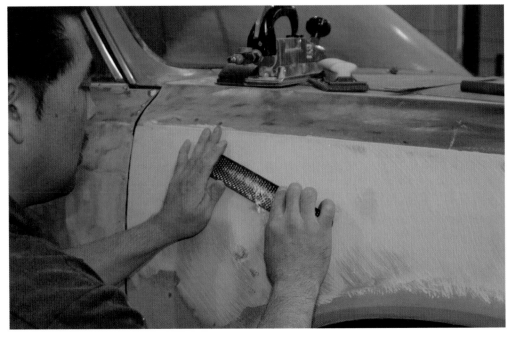

The application process involves dipping the car body into a large tank of liquid primer while an electrostatic charge is sent through the body of the car, which alters the chemical properties of the liquid. The body is then cured in large ovens at about 350 degrees F until it is fully cured. This process delivers primer to every square inch of the metal's surface and requires no sanding. There is no better method of covering the base metal of the car for extended protection but, unfortunately, it is almost impossible to perform this process without dipping the car in a large tank. *This is why the best substrate to apply paint over is a properly sanded factory paint job.*

Zinc chromate primers are basically used for aluminum or in any application where dissimilar metals are used together and have the potential of creating electrolysis. This type of primer acts as an insulator that prevents the metal from carrying a charge from one alloy to the next. Zinc chromate is used in many aircraft and marine applications and on exotic aluminum-bodied cars.

An anti-chip primer is the soft coating that is applied on many cars along the rocker panel area and in the wheel wells. It normally cannot be applied over bare metal. Its sole purpose is to absorb the impact of road debris that might otherwise chip the paint. It is normally applied with a rough surface texture.

Surfacers are simply the primers that are applied over the base primer and are also intended as fillers when applied in very thick *high-build* coats. Surfacers are formulated to provide excellent bonding with primer. But before I get too far ahead into the topic of coatings, we need to get back to basic bodywork and talk about something that I *really* like to talk about: tools!

One of the handiest tools we have is this portable Bend Pak lift. We simply slide it under a car, and with 110 volts (standard plug) lift the car to a workable height. No more back problems from bending over while sanding rockers!

Once filed down and sanded, the fender is ready for a coat of primer. Primer is sprayed onto the panel to fill small imperfections.

The fender is primed and Brian moves to the next panel and starts over with the air file. As he finishes one panel, he moves to the next one. His finishing bodywork will include wet sanding with finer grits of paper, followed by more priming and prepping the car for paint.

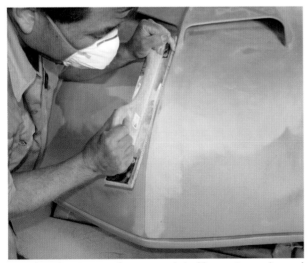

Even though we seem to have every air tool known to man in our shop, we still use the long boards for finishing the surface of a custom car. There is no tool that replaces the human feel for shaping a compound curve on a car.

Chapter Two

Tools!

This little paint thickness tester (PosiTest DFT) will tell you the paint thickness on a car that is made of steel or aluminum. It will help you decide if the car needs to be stripped because the paint is too thick or if there is too much filler in any area.

This '27 "T" had a small wrinkle in the fender, which was a bit hard to reach with a conventional hammer. The Slide Sledge was utilized for a well-placed hit that removed the wrinkle with one hit. This saved having to remove the front wheel for what amounted to a three-second repair job.

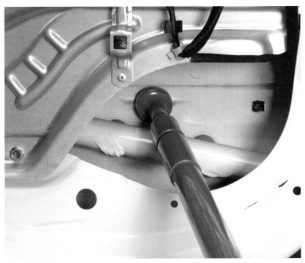

Try this with a hammer sometime. A hammer can't get into some areas on cars, but the Slide Sledge can.

A Slide Sledge is the converse of the slide hammer. The Slide Sledge is for pounding, while the slide hammer is for pulling. With the Slide Sledge you can place precision hits exactly where you want them.

Everything You'll Need and Everything You'll Want

I love talkin' tools because I love tools and this business allows me to buy and own tools, lots of them. As a matter of fact, I think I may have more tools than I'll ever be able to use in this lifetime, but it's a great feeling knowing that I have them. Brian takes pride in having all the tools he needs to do any job. Actually, his towering Snap-on KRL1023 Series combination top & bottom roll cab (the largest

setup on four wheels) contains enough equipment for the whole crew to work out of when the need arises. Whether it's bodywork, painting, fabrication, electrical work, writing and editing, or high-resolution digital photography, he has the right tools. One thing that I can't quite comprehend is that for the past few years, it seems that every person showing up in my shop claiming to have experience and wanting to work has very few tools, or none at all. You can't have experience, or hope to get any experience, if you don't have tools.

Many of the colors and coatings that once came only in cans and had to be mixed are now in rattle cans, making them much easier to apply.

Most of the products you need will be available through reputable companies like Eastwood, and yes, they still have some products in cans that can be sprayed or brushed. Most paints have to be shipped by ground, so order ahead of time to avoid delays.

A shear cuts a thin strip of metal out of a sheet as you move the cutter along, while a nibbler cuts hundreds or thousands of little chunks of metal at a time. Don't kneel down on the chunks or you will be picking them out of your knees with tweezers.

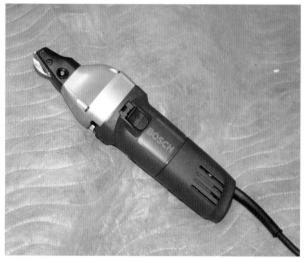

Bosch makes a great 110-volt electric slot cutting sheer for cutting metal. It is a good alternative to an air-powered sheer if you don't have an air supply handy. Some people simply prefer electric over air. I use both, depending on the job and where I am in the shop.

What these guys don't realize is that a nice toolbox and a set of good quality tools makes a statement. It says that you can handle the job and you do so with pride.

Automotive tools are to guys what shoes, clothes and jewelry are to women; we can't have enough of them. I know guys who can hardly wait to show off a new tool that he just bought. In the autobody repair business, tools are a sign of a professional that has experience, and even though having a lot of tools is not a surefire indication that a guy can handle a job, the fact that he has tools is certainly a step in the right direction.

It's said that the difference between man and animal is that man uses tools and animals don't. While not entirely true (monkeys *have* been known to use tools), I will offer an alternative euphemism: "The difference between man and animal is that some animals may use tools to live, but real men live to use tools." So if you're feeling a little bit guilty about your lack of tools or tool savvy, then this chapter is written especially for you! Every tool that you see here is what I feel should be in every serious body repairman's box.

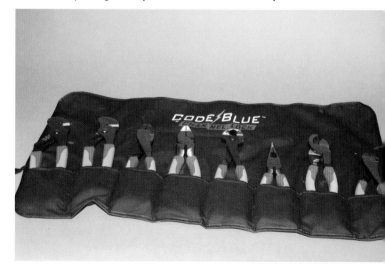

Channel Lock makes a nice new set of tools called Code Blue that feature ergonomic grips.

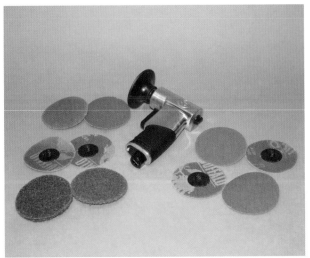

Right-angle sanders and grinders are "must-have" tools for getting into tight areas. With the new twist-lock mechanism, it is very quick and easy to change back and forth between sanding and grinding disks.

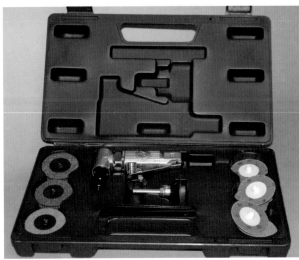

Some of these sanding kits come with scuff pads of varying abrasive potential. They can be used for removing rust, paint or metal just by changing the abrasive.

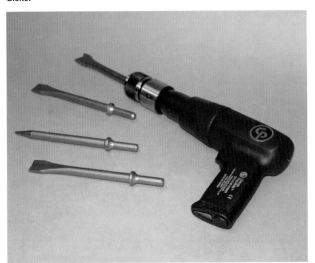

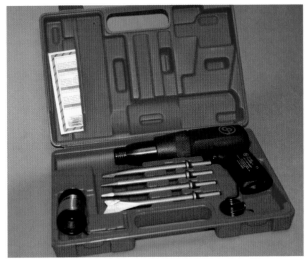

It's amazing how many people have never used an air hammer for cutting metal. Some of the guys in my shop were blown away the first time we pulled one out and started cutting metal with it. It is fast and easy and will start a cut in the center of a panel if needed. It's a good idea to have a set of hearing protectors handy for this. The air hammer is very loud.

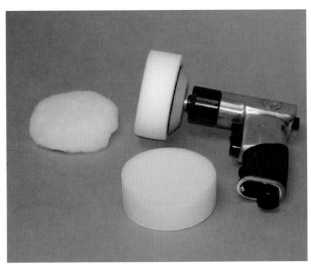

Small right-angle attachments are now available that have soft pads for buffing hard-to-reach areas on your car or motorcycle. This CP tool is actually a mini orbital buffer.

The biggest advantage the nibbler has over shears is the ability to start a cut from a small hole in the center of a panel. With a shear you will need to start on the edge of the sheet or from a much larger hole in the panel.

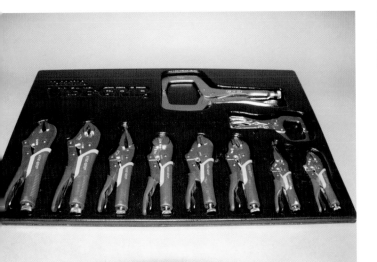

Vise Grip is now in the ergonomic handle-making business as well, making the Vice Grip a lot easier to use and grip when you have oily hands. It also makes them easier to spot in the shop and a lot better looking.

The straight cut-off tool accepts an abrasive cut-off wheel and can be used for everything from cutting a body panel to cutting a piece of bar stock.

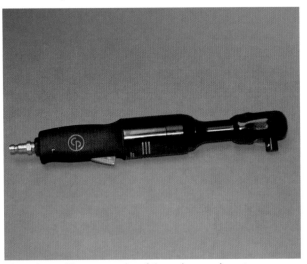

Air ratchets will save you a lot of time when you have to remove fenders and do not have the room to swing a wrench.

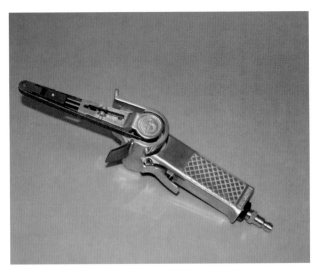

When these small belt grinders first came out they were not worth the metal they were made out of, but over the years the manufacturers have improved them to the point that I have about five of them and use them all the time.

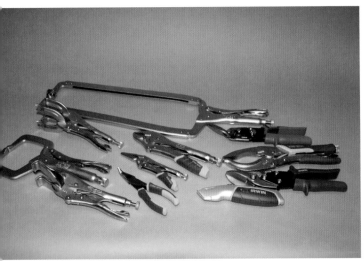

An assortment of clamps and cutters are helpful for making small "patch panels" for minor rust repair.

This is an example of either an air-powered grinder, or a buffer, depending on the rpm of the unit. Grinders run at a much higher speeds than buffers. If you try to use a grinder for buffing your car, you will likely burn the paint, ruin the pad, or both.

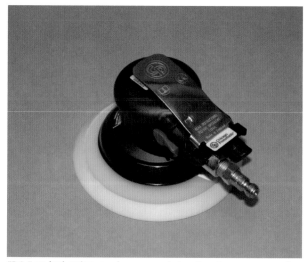

"DA," or dual-action, sanders are made by almost every pneumatics company there is. It's no surprise that the more they cost, the better they usually are.

I found this little jewel of a tool, at a Snap-On tool show in Las Vegas, Nevada. (Yes, I go to tool shows!) And when I saw the demo of it cutting and removing paint and rust, I just had to have one. You can add a rubber wheel to it and remove stickers without harming base paint.

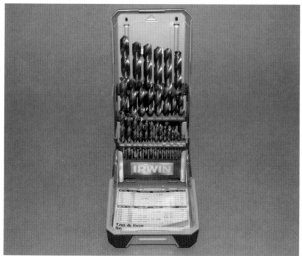

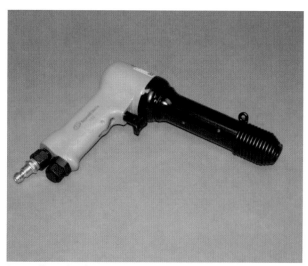

A good drill set or index is a must for bodywork. A higher-quality set like this Irwin set will last many years — if you don't loan them out to anyone.

Ingersoll Rand makes a very high-end air chisel.

Almost all major body damage results in some frame repair being required. For such repairs, we have a "Quick Stick" frame machine from USA Tools. This little portable machine will handle most damage that has occurred to your average frame from an unprovoked attack by another car, pole or tree.

MIG and TIG welders are scattered throughout our shop and used daily on everything from frame welding to simple patch panels on rusty fenders. If you are on a limited budget I would start with the purchase of the MIG welder first, and later add a plasma cutter, then a TIG welder. The MIG seems to be used a lot more and is a lot faster and easier to use than the TIG.

Impact wrenches are the easiest way to remove wheels. This Snap-On model works very well. Every lug nut we have ever tried it on, even the stubborn ones, have come off with ease.

When we built the real cars for the CARS tour, we made the bodies out of plastic. But even though they were plastic instead of metal, many of the principles were the same. A lot of the tools are also the same, such as this Chicago Pneumatic air chisel we used for cutting and narrowing a fender.

This area at the back of Mater's cab was ground down using a small right angle grinder, just as on a metal body. This is an area where we bonded two parts together and are getting ready to mold the seam in with SEM glue and Evercoat body filler.

On another area on Mater we added a strip of aluminum below the seam and then riveted the two body parts together. We then used a body adhesive from SEM that bonded the two parts into one. This was also a great place to use the cordless drills. With all the people working on the truck at one time we would have had cords or hoses spread out everywhere if we used 110-volt tools or air tools.

Craftsman makes a nice universal tool set with battery-powered driver that includes nut drivers, drills and an assortment of other tools for general work around the shop.

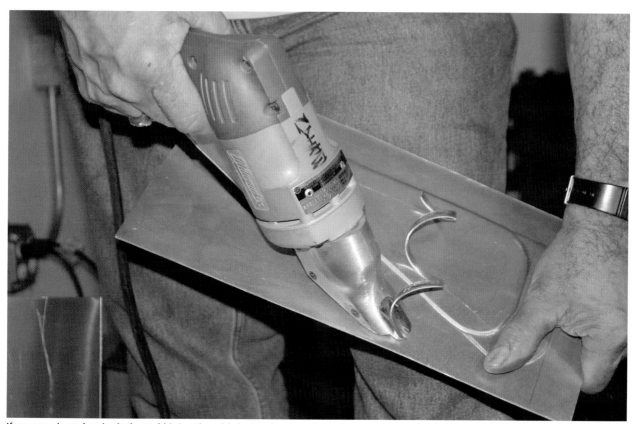

If you use air or electric air shears (this is a three-blade shear) on aluminum, be sure to spray the aluminum with WD-40 every so often to keep the blades from binding. It helps to use WD-40 on steel, as well, just to make the cuts go smoother.

Get a good-quality Milwaukee right-angle grinder and use it for life. I have started buying the better brands and saved the time and gas money running out each week to replace the cheaper tools. This being said, sometimes the lower-priced tools are not a bad investment, if you only plan on using it once or need to loan it out.

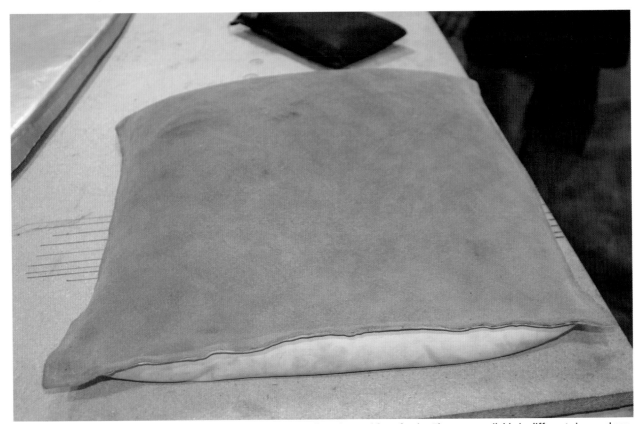

A beater bag, or sand bag, is a nice item for shaping metal into a small patch panel for a fender. These are available in different sizes and can be filled with sand or lead shot.

Once you try an extended-reach cutoff tool like this one from Ingersoll Rand, you will never want to be without one. These things are not a toy and cut through welds and rusty bolts with ease.

A spray gun, or two, are required for body repair and paint. This is the last place you want to skimp and buy a cheap product, that is, unless you like sanding runs and buffing out dull dry spots. The ideal setup is to have one gun just for primer, a gun for color and a gun for clear. This will prevent cross contamination of the paint and colors.

Slick Sand is a polyester primer surfacer that will fill small imperfections well and sand smooth with little effort once it is set. Be sure to wear a respirator when spraying primers.

Tools!

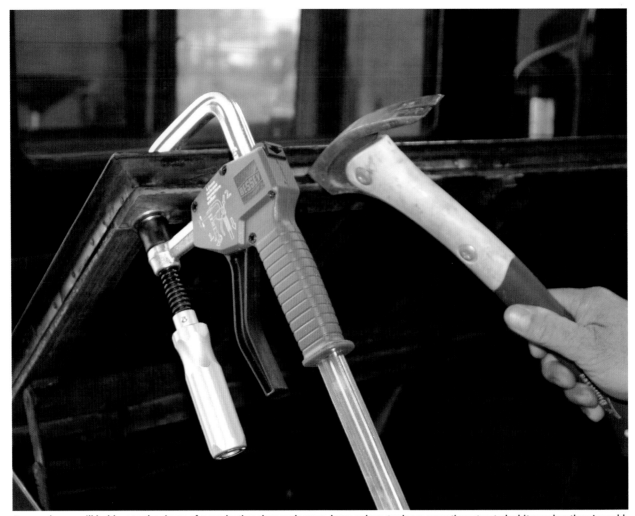

Bessey clamps will hold up to the rigors of a production shop such as we have, where tools are sometimes treated a bit rougher than I would like.

A cheese grater, or "Sure-form" file, is the best way to take filler down to shape shortly after it hardens and just before it totally sets up. This will save you hours of sanding, but timing is still critical. You have a small window of time to use this tool after you apply the filler, or you might as well just use the sandpaper because the filler will be too hard to grate.

The Morgan Nokker comes in a steel box with all the attachments to handle most of your pulling needs. A variety of sizes are available.

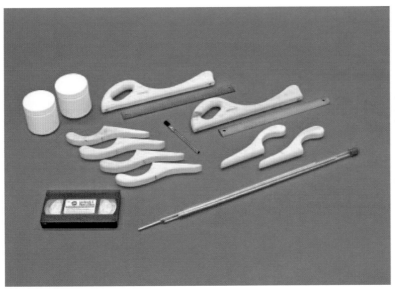

Eastwood makes a lead-working kit with all the support tools you will need for working in lead. Our shop is also producing a new video on lead working. If you are starting a classic restoration and you need to use lead for the repair, this is a great kit to get. It comes with its own video.

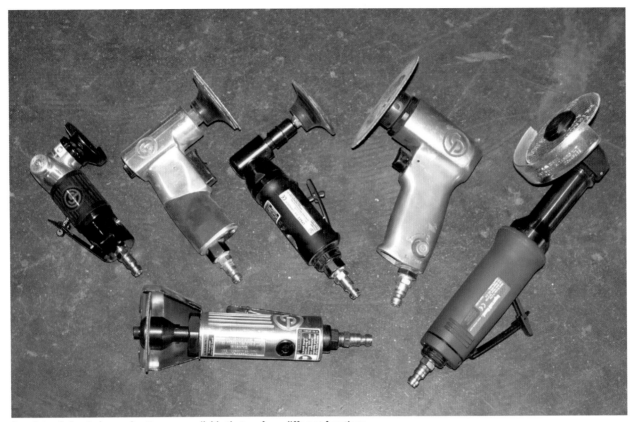

A variety of air grinders and cutters are available that perform different functions.

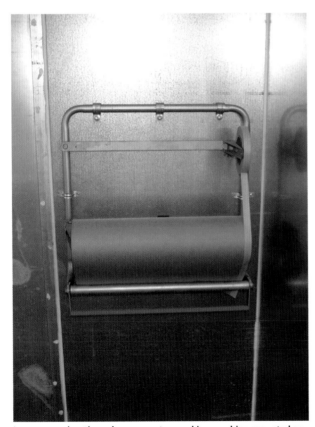

In our spray booth we have an extra masking machine mounted on the wall for last-minute masking jobs. We keep this one very clean. This way, we do not have to bring one in to the booth that could be covered in dust and dirt.

For the shop, we have the portable masking machine that we can roll to the car as we mask it off.

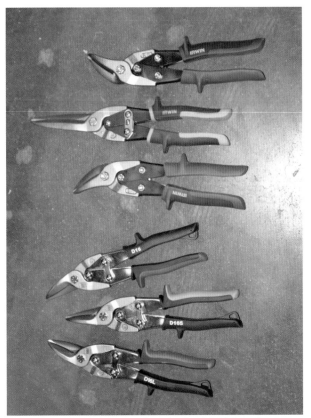

Irwin and Bessey make top-quality snips for right, left and center cutting.

Hutchins offers quite a few orbital and straight-line sanders. The top sander in this photo is used for shaping and rapid removal of filler. The bottom tool is another of Hutchins' many orbital sanders.

An infrared lamp will speed up drying of primer, fiberglass and fillers on cold days.

A two-bay charger such as this one by Bosch is a definite time saver. It is a good idea to have spare batteries ready and charged as you work. I normally have about four extras.

The Bodyworker's Tool Directory

Twenty years ago, shopping for body repair and metal-working tools meant having to know exactly what you wanted and then going out and finding it. Oftentimes that required a whole day of driving from store to store, thumbing through catalog after catalog, then placing an order and waiting. Today, thanks to the Internet, everything from a basic hammer to the latest mini grinder from Chicago Pneumatic to a replacement Blue Core battery for your cordless Bosch drill can be found, researched and ordered with nothing more than a few clicks of the mouse button! You can visit the many tool manufacturers listed on the following pages for a look at their online catalogs, or you can make a purchase online from companies such as Eastwood Tools, Auto Body Toolmart, or Tools USA. If you still have trouble finding what you need, just click on your favorite search engine and type the name of the tool that you are looking for.

The companies listed here are the ones that make most of the tools that you see throughout this book. From one do-it-yourselfer to another, these are the ones that I prefer and recommend.

Back supports are made by many companies. This is the one we use made by Back-A-Line. The company also makes knee pads for times when you are going to be working on your hands and knees.

Ajax Tool Works (air chisels, hand and power tool accessories)
10801 Franklin Avenue
Franklin Park, IL 60131
Phone: 800-323-9129
Web site: www.ajaxtools.com

Back-a-line, Inc. (knee pads, back support belts)
644 11th Avenue
San Francisco, CA 94118
Phone: 800-905-2225
Web site: www.backaline.com

Bend-pak Inc. (automotive lifts)
1645 Lemonwood Drive
Santa Paula, CA USA 93060
Local phone: 805-933-9970, toll-free phone: 800-253-2363
Web site: www.bendpak.com

Bessey Tools North America (clamps, snips, hammers)
1165 Franklin Blvd., Unit G / P.O. Box 490
Cambridge, ON N1R 5V5
Phone: 519-621-7240
Web site: www.americanclamping.com

Bosch Tools and Accessories (cordless and electric power tools)
Phone: 877-BOSCH-99
Web site: www.boschtools.com

Channellock, Inc. (pliers, cutters)
1306 South Main Street
Meadville, PA 16335
Phone: 800-724-3018
Web site: www.channellock.com

Chicago Pneumatic (pneumatic power tools)
Web site: www.chicagopneumatic.com

Craftsman (power and hand tools, tool storage, compressors)
Web site: www.sears.com

ESAB (welding equipment and consumables)
Web site: www.esab.com

Eastwood Tools (autobody, restoration and metalworking tools)
263 Shoemaker Road
Pottstown, PA 19464
Toll-free phone: 800-345-1178
Web site: www.eastwood.com

In-line air files are great time savers. They are made in different lengths, and you will want to use the longest one you can fit on a panel.

E.P. Industries, Inc. (restoration/metal fabrication tools, how-to DVDs/videos)
2305 Utah Avenue
El Segundo, CA 90245
Phone: 310-643-8515
Web site: www.epindustries.com

Hutchins Manufacturing Company (pneumatic sanders and accessories)
49 North Lotus Avenue
Pasadena, CA 91107
Phone: 626-792-8211
Web site: www.hutchinsmfg.com

Ingersoll Rand (pneumatic power tools)
Web site: www.irtools.com

INNOVA—Emissive Energy Corp. (L.E.D. flashlights)
135 Circuit Drive
N. Kingstown, RI 02852
Phone: 401-294-2030
Web site: www.innova.com

Irwin Industrial Tools (Vise Grips)
Web site: www.irwin.com

Lincoln Electric Company (welding equipment)
22801 St. Clair Avenue
Cleveland, OH 44117
Phone: 216-481-8100
Web site: www.lincolnelectric.com

Milwaukee Electric Tool Corp. (cordless and electric power tools)
13135 W. Lisbon Road
Brookfield, WI 53005
Toll-free phone: 800-729-3878
Web site: www.milwaukeetool.com

Morgan Manufacturing, Inc. (Morgan "Nokker" slide hammers, accessories)
521 2nd Street
Petaluma, CA 94952
Phone: 800-423-4692
Web site: www.morganmfg.com

Motor Guard Corporation (Magna Spot welders)
580 Carnegie Street
Manteca, CA 95337
Phone: 209-239-9191
Web site: www.motorguard.com

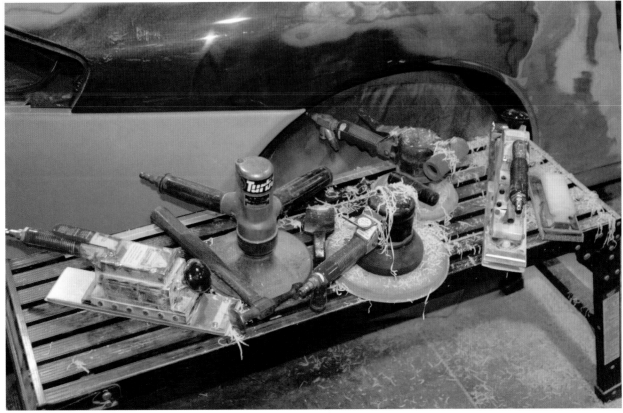

Here is a typical assortment of tools we use on fender repair and repaint.

National Detroit Inc. (pneumatic sanding, grinding and buffing tools)
P.O. Box 2285
Rockford, IL 61131
Phone: 815-877-4041
Web site: www.nationaldetroit.com

P.B.E. Specialties (paint and body equipment)
13801 Kolter Road
Spencerville, OH 45887
Phone: 888-997-7416

Ranger Products (floor jacks, stands, lifts and tool storage)
1645 Lemonwood Drive
Santa Paula, CA USA 93060
Local phone: 805-933-9970, toll-free phone: 800-253-2363
Web site: www.rangerproducts.com

Ringers Gloves (work gloves, shoes)
335 Science Drive
Moorpark, CA 93021
1-800-421-8454
Web site: www.ringersgloves.com

Slide Sledge (sliding hammer)
2500 W. Higgins Road
Hoffman Estates, IL 60195
Phone: 800-276-0311
Web site: www.slidesledge.com

Snap-on (auto repair tools and storage)
Web site: www.snapon.com

Standard Tools and Equipment (automotive spray booths, body repair tools)
4810 Clover Road
Greensboro, NC 27405
Toll-free phone: 800-451-2425
Web site: www.toolsusa.com

Tru-line Laser Alignment
8231 Blaine Road
Blaine, WA 98230
Phone: 800-496-3777
Web site: www.tru-line.net

Chapter Three

Body Repair Materials

Chemicals consist of solvents, binders and additives, many of which are harmful if inhaled. Use a mask when working with any type of chemicals. Shown here are the paint prep, guide coat and acid etch primer chemicals we work with daily.

Metal Ready and Marine Clean are used for removing rust and prepping the metal for paint. They are made by POR 15. Eastwood has Silver Rust Encapsulator for the same purpose.

Slick Sand is a polyester primer surfacer that fills and builds up low spots.

A can of Anti Splatter will help you get rid of the little BB's that stick to everything surrounding a weld. A shot of this and the balls just roll off. We also spray our nozzles with it every so often to keep them clean.

The proper application and skillful shaping of a body filler, whether it be lead or plastic, will allow you to fill and blend repaired or patched areas of a body panel so that the repair is completely undetectable — and stays undetectable. Generally speaking, the main materials used for performing body repairs include three common automotive products: plastic filler, lead or body solder, and fiberglass. Sounds simple so far, right? Well, a quick look into any product catalog of repair materials will tell you differently. There are so many types, formulations and brands of plastic filler materials alone that it is impossible to cover everything here in one small chapter. Is Evercoat filler better than those from U.S.C., Dynatron Bondo, Marson, 3M or the paint manufacturers such as PPG filler? And if you choose to go with a particular brand of filler such as Evercoat, how do you know which one of the more than two dozen Evercoat fillers to use?

For the average guy attempting to learn some basic body repair techniques, this can get into a pretty mind-boggling experience. So rather than add to the confusion, my objective here will be to break down the topic of body repair and help you understand what to use and how to use it. I'll try to do this by showing you what materials we use here at my shop, Customs By Eddie Paul, and how we use it.

Before I branch off into brands and formulas for the various materials though, let us first take a look at what falls into the category of body repair materials:

➤ **Lead:** Sometimes referred to as body solder, lead is undoubtedly the first and foremost choice of purists, old school repairmen and traditional customizers. For all practical purposes, lead has all but been replaced by resin-based fillers. Ever since the late 1960s and early '70s, lead use in both repair work and customizing has been gradually decreased, and if it weren't for the enthusiast publications and books (such as this one), there would be absolutely

Body filler can have some nasty fumes. Use ventilation — at least a fan — or work outside if possible when applying filler.

Painting a car involves the use of a lot of chemicals, many of which can be hazardous to your health. Don't tackle this type of work without at least minimal safety equipment such as a fan of mask.

Body filler "flashes off" as it dries, so try to avoid breathing the fumes directly. Just walk away as you let it set up.

Evercoat makes a few different fillers for a variety of applications.

Rust removal chemicals can also be dangerous to young lungs. Be cautious with all of them and take the proper safety measures.

no public endorsement for the lost art of lead work and its materials. But thanks to companies such as Eastwood, lead-working tools and materials are still readily available, as are the newer lead-free kits.

➤ **Plastic filler:** First of all, "Bondo" is a plastic filler, but not all plastic filler is Bondo. Bondo is a trade name of The Bondo Corporation that has become the generic moniker among "mudslingers" for any material used to fill a dent. Just about everybody I know uses the term "Bondo" in place of plastic filler, regardless of what company actually makes the filler being used. For the sake of the Evercoat company, who makes all of the filler materials that we use in my shop, I'll try to refrain from doing so here and stick to the real generic term: plastic filler. I can't really explain why each manufacturer of plastic filler makes so many variations of the product. I'm sure that there are logical reasons for this such as cost, quality, textures, leveling effect and workability.

➤ **Glaze:** The process of shaping either lead or

Even when we are pouring paint we turn on the spray booth fans for ventilation.

Eastwood offers most of the coatings you'll ever need for restoring, priming and painting a car. The coatings come in handy spray cans.

plastic filler results in heavy sanding grit marks and tiny pinholes. Sanding marks, pinholes and any other minute imperfections must be filled, and the best material for this step is a catalyzed glaze. Some body workers use an acrylic spot putty for this process. A non-catalyzed spot putty is nothing more than an acrylic primer in paste form. Suffice it to say that we do not use non-catalyzed putty at Customs By Eddie Paul.

Metal-based filler: Perhaps the best alternative to metal finishing or using lead as a filler is a product such as Evercoat's Metal-To-Metal (MTM). MTM is an aluminum-filled moisture-proof repair filler for metal surfaces that provides excellent corrosion resistance for the metal substrate. The sanding quality of MTM is comparable to plastic filler, meaning that it sands easily to a fine featheredge.

Flexible filler: When rubber bumper covers first came out back in the '70s, repair methods were few and good materials even fewer. Today, there are several top-

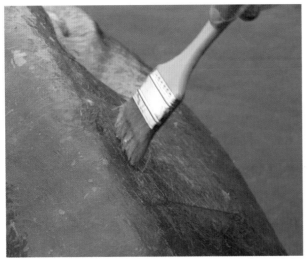

Fiberglass is simple to apply and work with, but will make you itchy and miserable if you get it on your skin during sanding. I really haven't found a good way to avoid getting the dust on my skin, but a mask during grinding is an absolute requirement.

Fiberglass particles become airborne when sanded and can get into your lungs if you don't have a mask. We use disposable brushes and light latex gloves even when brushing on the resin.

quality flexible parts repair materials available, and the compatibility with late-model bumper cover plastic has improved tremendously.

Fiberglass-reinforced filler: A good compromise between the strength and moisture-resistance of lead or metal-based filler and standard plastic filler is a fiberglass-reinforced filler such as Evercoat's Everglass, Tiger Hair or Kitty Hair. Fiberglass-reinforced filler has workability similar to plastic, but with increased strength and moisture resistance.

Fiberglass: Not much has changed with fiberglass materials. Polyester resin, catalyst, and fiberglass matte and cloth are still the standard materials.

Adhesives: Over the years, the use of composites for body panels and trim has grown. So, too, has the need for special adhesives. Different plastics, flexibility, set-up time and even colors have created a large market full of products

from companies such as SEM and 3M.

Rubberized undercoating: No panel repair is complete until the backside is treated to a rubberized undercoating. Aside from the aesthetic, there are many reasons to invest in a can or two of rubberized undercoating for repair work. It's also a good idea to use this product on exposed panels if there is no factory coating. Evercoat offers a brushable and sprayable coating that seals exposed metal from the elements and also acts as a sound deadener.

Seam sealer: The application of a seam sealer is something that often gets overlooked during a repair. Just about every panel that can be replaced, such as a door skin, quarter panel, core support, or a tail light panel will have seams, or edges, that must be sealed to prevent trapped water from rusting the metal.

Learning how to properly apply repair materials is just as important as knowing how to reshape metal and use

Eddie Paul's Paint & Bodywork Handbook

The Chemistry of Molding

Plastic filler is the mainstay of auto body repair work. Without it, even the simplest door ding couldn't be fixed economically. Plastic fillers were developed to take the place of lead. There are some long-standing misconceptions about the use of plastic filler that I feel need to be put to rest. First of all, "Bondo," which is plastic filler, is actually a trade name of the Bondo Corporation and not a generic term even though many people use it as such. There are several companies that manufacture top-quality plastic fillers, including Evercoat, the brand that I use exclusively in my shop. The second issue concerns quality, something that all of us strive for. To sum it up in one sentence: Plastic filler will last the life of the car as long as it is applied correctly over a properly prepared surface.

Plastic filler is a polyester-based substance that requires the addition of a catalyst for it to harden. The amount of catalyst can vary depending on ambient temperature, so the best way to determine the proper ratio is to mix up a small test batch and note the shade of color of the catalyzed mix. If you use different brands of filler, the catalyst might be red or blue. The reason for having a colored catalyst is to provide a visual indicator that tells when your filler and catalyst are thoroughly mixed. When a batch is mixed, the mixture should have a uniform color with no swirls. In my experience, there is no difference between the different catalyst colors, with one exception: the red catalyst has a tendency to bleed through primer and sealer coats and discolors the final finish of certain light colors. So as a general rule, I avoid using red catalyst with plastic filler.

Over the years, plastic filler technology has progressed to the point that today's fillers are very light weight and have a self-leveling consistency. Also, the workability of today's plastic filler has improved by leaps and bounds. The Evercoat line of fillers offer easy sanding with minimal build-up and clogging on the sandpaper. We use their Z-Grip, Rage and Rage Gold for general purpose work, Extreme Rage for covering slight imperfections and skim-coating, Metal Glaze and Poly Glaze for filling those tiny pinholes and sanding scratches, and Everglass for rust-sensitive areas. Everglass is a waterproof fiberglass-reinforced filler that is both stronger and harder than standard filler.

Repairing plastic body parts, such as urethane bumper covers or rear deck lid spoilers, may require the use of a special plastic repair material. There are several types of products available from SEM and 3M for bonding, filling and glazing plastic parts. Depending on the operation that you are performing, you may want to read up on the latest plastic repair materials in those companies' product catalogs. Plastic repair materials are formulated to provide strong adhesion with an adequate amount of flexibility to prevent cracking. It should be noted that parts made from rigid plastic such as ABS could be repaired with flexible or standard plastic filler materials.

auto body tools, and is essential to becoming a skilled body repair person. There are other materials and chemicals used in the repair process, but the fillers will be the primary focus of this chapter. I'll get into undercoat and topcoat materials (primers, sealers and paints) later on.

Lead vs. Plastic

I am fairly certain that whichever side I choose to take here will anger some, while others will thank me for going public with it. I have more than 30 years worth of experience with both lead and plastic fillers. Over the course of that time, I've performed every conceivable type of repair on just about every type of vehicle, from concept cars to Army tanks.

Like most in the field of automotive body repair, my beginnings are humble, having learned from my dad the method of applying lead to body panels and shaping with a vixen file. As a teen I worked at a local shop that specialized in classic car restorations before opening my first business in El Segundo, California. To get things started, I took on any and all jobs that I could get, which explains why my clientele ranged from scruffy bikers riding in on their Harleys, to luxury car owners in their suits and ties, to Hollywood movie producers. The chopper work was plentiful but low paying; building cars for movies was lucrative but few and far between.

At the time, it seemed as though my bread and butter work might come from classic and high-end auto body repair, so I concentrated my efforts on looking for that type of work. I landed all of the body and restoration work from a company in nearby Santa Monica, California, called Automotive Classics Car Company. As their name implied, they dealt strictly in the sale of classics that included marques such as Bugatti, Duesenberg, Packard, Lotus and Shelby Cobra. The company's one and only requirement was that all body repair work be done using lead. But for 99 percent of the "regular" work, I used plastic filler.

Old-school customs were often referred to as lead sleds, and for good reason; they're low to the ground, not because of the suspension modification, but because of the amount of lead shoveled on them and weighing them down. Whether it be plastic or lead, you should never put either on too thick just to finish a job. Spend the extra time to bring the metal to a closer tolerance of the finished product then add a bit of filler to clean it up and make the surface smooth.

Chapter Four

Welding Skills

Eddie Paul's Paint & Bodywork Handbook

We work with most of the welding companies — Miller, ESAB, and Lincoln — as well as the companies that make plasma cutters, such as Hypertherm. They all have different features that make each of them unique.

We use a copper plate many times for backing up a weld. The weld won't stick to the copper.

Anti Spatter can help eliminate that weld splatter and keep material from sticking to the area that surrounds the weld, including the welding table. Most welding shops sell it in 16-oz. cans.

One of the essential skills of body repair is the ability to attach two pieces of metal together. While this can be accomplished with rivets or adhesives, the most common and preferred method is *welding*. Welding is the process of heating metal up to its melting point, allowing the fusion of molecules between two separate sheets.

There are a number of ways to achieve the required heat required to weld metal. One way is by igniting a combination of flammable gases; another is through the use of electricity to create an arc by grounding the rod (or wire), or by creating an arc with an electrode to melt the metal then adding a filler rod of a similar material to the open gap. Fortunately for those who are starting out in autobody repair, welding is not difficult to learn. Once you acquire some fundamental techniques, you'll find that they're applicable to all forms of welding. You'll also discover that familiarity with the different types of welding equipment is just as important as knowing how to use them.

As with any skill, there are many ways to weld incorrectly, but only a few ways to get the job done right. As a shop owner, I sometimes find myself having to make generalizations when it comes to evaluating a person's body repair or fabricating skills. For instance, I can often tell if a person is better at welding or better at reshaping metal simply by watching how that person goes about a particular repair job. If the damaged panel they are working on is quickly cut away in favor of a patch panel or a skin, then chances are that the ability to reshape a panel is not as strong as the ability to cut and weld one into place. On the other hand, if the repairman reaches into his toolbox and pulls out a hammer and dolly, then I know that, while he may be an accomplished welder, he also possesses the ability to reshape a damaged panel without replacing it. But like I said, this is a generalization and doesn't necessarily mean anything in the real world of basic body repair.

When I was in high school, I dreamed of becoming a

I often catch our guys tack welding by turning their head to one side as they pull the trigger on the MIG welder. This is not recommended!

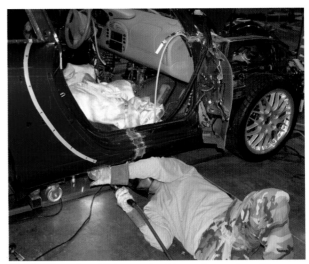

We often have to get into some hard-to-reach areas to weld. Fortunately, in this instance we only needed a small tack weld.

You can light up a welding area with small work lights sold at most hardware stores.

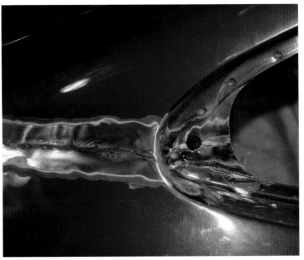

This MIG weld has been ground down after welding. The warpage has been kept to a minimum by the concentrated heat area of the MIG.

customizer but, unfortunately, there were no shop classes on that subject. Although I could care less about banging dents out of damaged fenders and doors, I signed up for the auto body shop class because it seemed like the closest thing to customizing. As it turned out, this was a pretty good career move for me because my shop teacher, knowing that I wanted to customize, came up to me during a welding segment and handed me an old tin can that had been cut in half. He placed it in front of me and said, "When you can fix this can, I will teach you a few customizing tricks." Well, it took quite a lot of practice for me to tame the torch, so to speak, into melting the metal just enough to weld a nice even bead around the can that did not warp or destroy the metal. About three weeks later, I walked up to the teacher and place the can on his desk, full of water. I said, "I'll take you up on that offer now."

So, the rest of that school year was spent staying after class learning to shape and bend metal, rolling pans, and making fender skirts and custom grilles. I learned that welding — the same kind of welding that I learned autobody shop — was a major part of customizing and fabrication. And even though I would never have to repair another tin can again, the lesson was well learned. Once I learned the basics of welding, I realized that I could get into other lines of work as well. I was able to help my dad out at his shop when he asked me to weld some overhead I-beams into place for a conveyer system he was building. I was young enough to climb up to the ceiling of his shop and weld while hanging by my legs wrapped around a beam. It wasn't a fun job, but I got really good at arc welding, which was another skill that I would be able to use as a customizer.

Tools For Welding and Cutting

As your welding skills develop, it becomes necessary to learn about and invest in the equipment. Selecting a

To finish the welding under the car, we put the car on our Bend Pak lift.

welder requires some careful thought on your part. Some things that you'll have to take into consideration are: your budget, the application, power availability. There are several manufacturers that offer a complete line of welders, but rather than taking up space by reviewing each and every machine available, I'll be able to provide a fairly wide cross-section of examples with a look at some of the welders that we use here in my shop. Since we handle everything from heavy production welding to light sheet-metal patch jobs with all types of metal, the welding equipment that I use covers just about every application that you will most likely encounter in a typical or not-so-typical repair job. The final choice all depends on your particular needs, application and source of power.

An auto body repair professional should be capable of using several types of welders. Versatility with your skills is critical because you never know what kind of repair situation you'll run up against. There's basic gas welding with an oxygen-acetylene torch. There's the arc welder (also called a "stick welder" or "buzz box." There's Heliarc (also called TIG, or tungsten-inert-gas welding). Last, but not least, is MIG (metal-inert-gas) welding. MIG welding is the body repair industry standard choice these days for many reasons, and this is the form of welding that I'll focus on here.

But first I'll digress a bit. Most of us are familiar with oxygen-acetylene gas welding, more commonly referred to as oxy-acetylene, or simply gas welding. This form of welding uses a mixture of two gases to produce a high-

This Lincoln TIG welder has simple settings and is easy to use.

temperature flame that can melt metals together or cut them apart. In this day and age, gas welders are used primarily for dismantling cars or other rough-cutting jobs, and for welding of heavy metal and machinery. Although basic gas welding is great for learning the fundamental skills, I do not recommend gas welding for bodywork except as a last resort. There are two good reasons for this. One is that gas welding can generate an excessive build up of heat, which

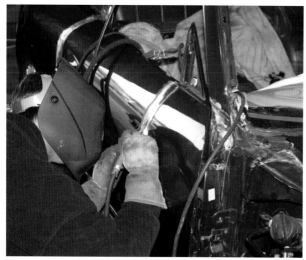

On Sally, we had to shorten the doors and re-weld them back together without warping them. Shannon decided to use TIG for this process.

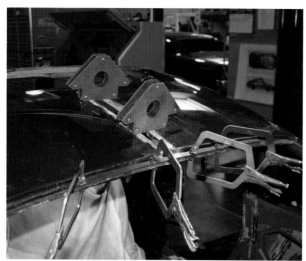

This is Sally from the movie *CARS*. We had to narrow the roof and re-weld it together again, which involved a bit of clamping with magnetic welding clamps to keep the panel alignment.

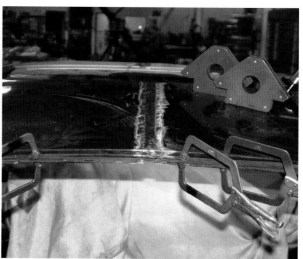

Clamping a piece of bar stock across the rear window pinch kept the roof aligned and the pinch flat and able to accept the rear window molding.

is the primary cause of panel warping. Another reason is the safety factor due to the open flame. Although some body shops still use oxy-acetylene to braze a door skin into place or to hot-shrink metal, this process has all but been replaced by MIG welding, as has the arc welder. The most common use of the gas torch in my shop is for annealing aluminum and steel.

Still, there are some viable reasons why you may want a gas welder for your shop or garage. For one, it's very portable because it does not require electricity. Secondly, the initial cost to set up an oxy-acetylene welder is fairly low (ranging between $100 to $300).

The drawbacks of gas welding generally outweigh the benefits, however. The two gas tanks are bulky, heavy, and you'll need to refill them (frequently if you do a lot of welding and cutting). From a practical standpoint, welding with oxy-acetylene tends to warp thin metals easily due to the amount of residual heat that it generates on a panel. In

other words, a gas welder can be difficult for a beginning welder to use.

The MIG (metal-inert gas) welder is the most versatile welder and by far the easiest to learn how to use. MIG welding uses an electric arc for fusion with a gun to feed the wire (hence the name "wide-feed" welder) to the metal and to strike the arc. The inert gas that I use for MIG in my shop is a mixture of 75 percent argon and 25 percent carbon-dioxide, which acts as a shield during the welding process and keeps the metal from oxidizing. Some of the small MIG welders can eliminate the shielding gas with a special wire called "flux core," which provides a similar effect as argon-CO2. Flux core wire welders can be referred to as gasless wire-feed welders, even though the flux produces the needed gas upon heating. The "gasless" refers more to the lack of a gas and tank. If you plan to take your welder "on the road" a lot, you may consider a MIG with flux-core wire. The simple addition of gas and a reverse of

Eddie Paul's Paint & Bodywork Handbook

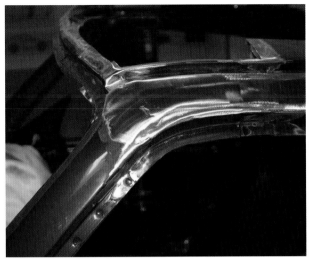

This corner was cut, shaped, welded and ground to metal in place with a MIG welder.

This is the right side of the roof. There were a lot of modifications with this job, and a lot of welding.

We performed a type of intermittent tack weld on this gas tank. It looked good enough for the finished product.

polarity will convert most of these gasless welders back to the bottle again.

MIG welders, whether 110-volt or 220-volt, come in different amperage ratings. The higher the amperage rating, the thicker the metal you can weld. I have used a 60-amp MIG welder, but its use is limited to thin sheet metals only. These smaller MIG welders usually require a standard 110-volt power source and are perfect for all types of body repair work.

The largest MIG welders that I have in my shop are rated at approximately 100 amps and are sufficient for welding both light and heavy metals. Welding equipment manufacturers claim that 100 amps is good for up to 1/2-inch steel, but I try to limit their use to metals with a thickness of no more than 3/8-inch steel (which will cover just about every automotive application that you'll encounter).

Body repair very rarely involves aluminum welding.

If you find yourself cutting and welding a body made of aluminum, the car is most likely a racecar or a high-end import. By the time you find yourself working on one of these, then hopefully you've advanced far beyond the stage of body repair basics! Aluminum welding can be performed with some MIG welders, but will require a "spool gun" (a special MIG gun with the spool of aluminum located at the gun). This is preferred over the normal wire fed from the machine because the softer aluminum wire often will get jammed up in the cable. Either way, the MIG welding technique for aluminum is almost as simple as welding steel.

Welding Gases and Wire

If you look inside a MIG welder, you won't find much in the way of complex machinery. What you will find is a replaceable spool of wire that feeds through the center

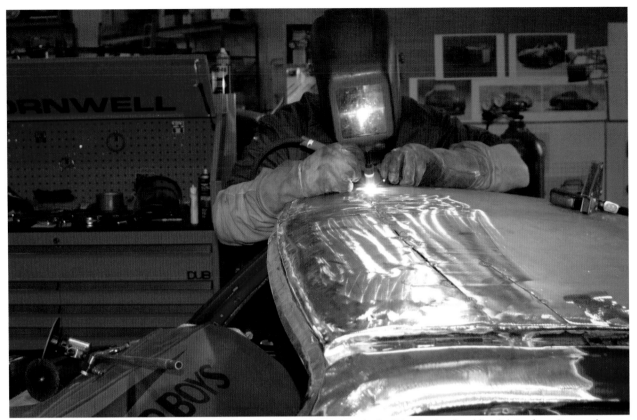

We filled this sunroof in with metal, which required shaping a piece of metal on the English wheel and welding it into place. Once again, we used a TIG welder to minimize warping.

of the "cable" connected to the gun. This cable also feeds welding current by way of the welding wire, supplies the shielding gas and transmits the trigger signal from the switch on the gun to the drive motor of the wire spool. When the gun is triggered, how fast the wire is pushed is determined by the setting you select. The MIG wire travels through copper tips at the outlet of the gun to keep it from fusing to the internal parts of the gun.

The biggest mistake welders make when they first learn to use the MIG is to pull the gun to form a continuous weld, or "bead." Pushing is not at all a normal feeling when welding (especially if you do a lot of "stick" welding, as I do), but pushing the weld keeps the gas in front of the arc and will make a much stronger weld with a uniform bead. Pushing instead of pulling will improve your welds by a bunch, as did mine. Besides, it is the correct way to weld with a MIG.

The type of gas that you use for either MIG or TIG welding depends upon the type of metal that you plan to weld. For basic body repair needs, you'll be welding mild steel. A few things to remember when setting up a welder are:

We often have to stretch or shorten frames and drive shafts. This isn't exactly basic bodywork, but definitely involves welding skills.

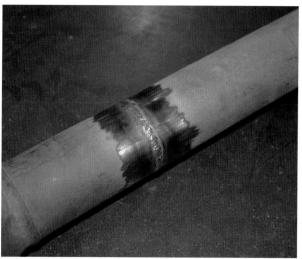

▼ A good welding machine, such as the Esab Migmaster 250 that we use most often in my shop, will have a handy reference chart located somewhere on the machine. This chart will provide all necessary information regarding machine settings (wire feed speed and amperage), the size filler wire to have on the spool (based on the thickness of the base metal to be welded), and the appropriate tip and nozzle sizes.

▼ Different gases are used for welding different materials. Mild steel MIG welding requires argon mixed with 25 percent carbon-dioxide (CO_2). Aluminum welding requires pure argon. Stainless steel welding requires argon

Quick Tip

For filling holes with a MIG welder, try backing the hole with a piece of copper sheet (about 2 x 2 inches) when you fill in the hole with weld. The welding wire will not stick to the copper, and once the copper is removed the hole will be filled, with the copper sheet acting as a backer or support for the molten metal. The copper will be hot, so be sure to use Vice Grips to hold the copper, not your hands. I have about 10 different shapes and sizes of copper sheet in my shop for just such a task.

Big bodywork jobs can require welding on sheet metal, thick steel bar, tubing or plate.

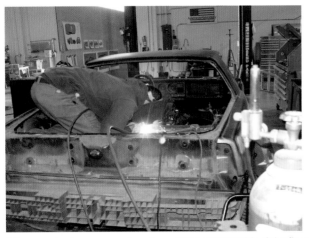

When we shorten a car, we have to weld the entire width of the floor to maintain structural integrity, just as you would have to do if you replaced a quarter panel on a stock car.

with 1 or 2 percent oxygen (O2).

◄ To keep it simple, set your welder up for the type of metal that you plan to weld most often, i.e. mild steel for basic bodywork.

If you can become a proficient welder, you might be able to pick up some extra money installing roll cages on racecars. Knowing how to weld tubing is a real asset, as well as good practice for other kinds of welding.

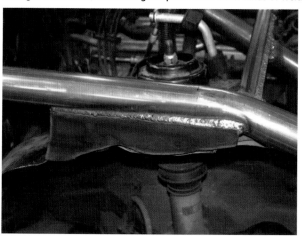

The plasma cutter has replaced the traditional oxygen-acetylene cutting torch in most shops today. Plasma cutters are faster, neater, safer and provide cleaner cuts than a torch.

We have several different sizes and types of plasma cutters in our shop. We use a Hypertherm Powermax 1000 in conjunction with a CNC PlasmaCAM for accurate, repeated cuts.

We also have a Hypotherm unit we can use by hand.

Plasma Cutting

No discussion about welding machines would be complete without touching on plasma cutters. Although most metal-cutting tasks that you'll encounter in body repair basics are best performed with a high-speed abrasive cut-off wheel, power saw or air hammer with a panel cutting bit, a growing number of people are becoming interested in plasma cutters.

The plasma cutter may sound like a high-tech piece of equipment, but it's actually quite a simple one. All matter takes on one of four forms: solid, liquid, gas, or plasma, depending on its temperature. When a solid is heated to its melting point, a liquid is formed. Heating the liquid to its point of evaporation turns it into gas. And heating gas to an extremely high temperature produces *plasma*. Most of the matter in our universe (the sun, for example) is plasma matter, but due to its extremely high temperature, the only plasma that you'll likely find on Earth is in a bolt of lightning or coming out of a plasma cutter nozzle!

So a plasma cutter is basically a machine that creates and harnesses the energy of a plasma arc to cut metal. Without getting into a boring lesson on the physics and science of plasma, suffice it to say that using a plasma cutter is the fastest and cleanest way to make flame cuts in metal without the residual heat generated by a conventional torch.

Because of the great amount of metal work that we do, my shop has several plasma cutters on hand ranging from small 110-volt models such as the Esab Handy Plasmarc 125 to the heavy-duty 220-volt Powercut 650 that can slice through a three-quarter-inch slab of steel like it was butter. Another good-quality plasma cutter is made by Hypertherm. My shop's PlasmaCAM CNC plasma cutter uses the Hypertherm Powermax 1250, which can cut up to a 1/4-inch-thick plate of steel. And for all-around hand cuts, we use the Hypertherm Powermax 1000 and 600 models. Like welding machines, plasma cutters range greatly in size and cost.

Using a plasma cutter is not only easy, but it's a lot of fun! Because of the accuracy of the plasma arc and the thick metal-cutting capability, this tool is a must for serious fabricators. In the right hands, it can be just as useful for cutting and installing patch panels, quarter panels and more.

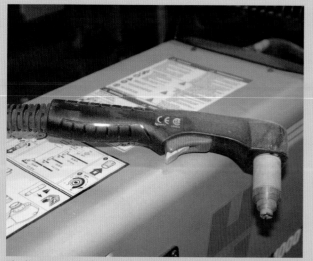

The business end of a plasma cutter is a handle. With the ground clamp attached to the metal, the trigger on the handle is pulled to strike the arc and begin cutting. Proper settings and correct tips must be used for specific jobs.

Plasma Cutting Tips

Bodywork often requires metal cutting and/or trimming. There are numerous tools available that are less expensive than a plasma cutting machine, but don't rule this tool out for the basics of body repair.

Although the plasma arc is extremely hot, one of the benefits of using a plasma cutter to cut thin sheet metal such as a body panel is that the residual heat buildup is minimal — probably less than the heat generated by cutting with an abrasive cut-off wheel. That means warping is also kept to a minimum, as is the damaging effect on a painted surface. The plasma cutter is also easy to use. When I first I picked up a plasma cutting torch, I was cutting steel like it was paper on my first try.

If you get into plasma cutting while performing any basic body repair, there are a few things to keep in mind to make your cuts accurate and safe.

- Always keep a fully charged fire extinguisher within reach.
- Always use a fire-resistant fiberglass or carbon fiber welding blanket to cover and protect anything within the range of the arc.
- Use caution when cutting undercoated or insulated panels. Many coatings are highly flammable.
- If you do not have access to the back side of a panel, use a cut-off wheel or a blade-type saw.
- Always wear the proper eye protection.
- Use a guide for cutting a straight line, rather than free-handing it.
- Do not allow the tip to contact the metal while cutting.

There are a number of ways to make a clean cut with a plasma cutter, even if you aren't proficient enough to free-hand it, like this. A guide can be especially helpful. Also, regulate the distance between the tip and the metal surface according to the manufacturer's instructions.

- When "punching" a hole in sheet metal with the plasma cutter, start the arc with the nozzle at about a 45-degree angle to the metal. After the hole is blown through, tilt the cutter down to a perpendicular position and start cutting. This is so the sparks and slag do not bounce back and fill the cutting nozzle with metal.
- As with a MIG welding machine, refer to the manufacturer's recommendations for settings and nozzle/tip selection for the metal that you are cutting.

Chapter Five

Repair or Replace?

Here is an example of the hidden damage that can result from an accident. This bent core support and inner structure will need to be repaired before a fender can be mounted.

This is an example of a rear quarter panel that can easily be repaired. In most cases, the rear quarter panels are easier to repair than to replace.

Replacing a pricey deck lid is usually faster than repairing it. If you have time to wait, you may be better off going the repair route, especially if you can do it yourself.

In a body shop, the decision of whether to repair or replace is almost always determined by cost or, more accurately, by *profit*. Whichever process is more economically feasible — either hammering out a damaged portion of a car, or simply replacing it — that's the way it must be done in order to remain profitable. For the weekend hobbyist or the do-it-yourselfer, profit should not be the bottom-line factor unless you're conducting a little side business to make a little extra money. But one thing to keep in mind here is that before profit comes the process of learning. You must have a total knowledge of repair work before you can entertain the idea of making money at it.

Once in a while, the choice of whether to repair or replace a damaged body part is predetermined when a particular make of car is just too old or too obscure to have any replacement parts available. All late models, and popular classic and high-performance cars, however, have an abundance of NOS (new original stock), used and reproduction pieces to choose from. Keep in mind, though, that not all reproductions are quality reproductions. I've seen some very poor quality repro parts out there that required a lot of work just to get them to fit.

The decision of whether to replace a damaged panel isn't always an easy one to make. When it comes to choosing the best avenue of repair, a lot of factors come into play, such as cost of material and parts, availability, originality, time and, for a beginner of body repair, your level of skill. In some cases, the need to replace the part is unavoidable due to the extent of the damage.

If a panel replacement is necessary, a new OEM (original equipment manufacturer) part is the first and most appealing option. In most cases, taking this route will allow you to maintain the originality of the vehicle, and you can be assured of getting a panel that fits perfectly. The downside to this is that a factory replacement part can be quite expensive, especially if the car is a limited edition or high-performance model. Depending on the make, model and year of the car, a new OEM replacement may not

The hood on this 1963 Thunderbird needs to be repaired — a replacement would far exceed the cost of the repair to this original piece.

be available. If this is the case, you might be able to find a reproduction piece or a good used one from a salvage yard.

The cost of repairing versus the cost of replacing is a fairly easy comparison to make, especially for those of us with access to the Internet. Once you can establish a baseline cost for replacing a panel, you can use that figure as the basic budget for making your repair. If you are venturing out on your first attempt at body repair, chances are you'll need to invest in some tools and supplies that will exceed the cost of a new replacement panel.

The Economics of Body Repair

For a lot of us, the primary motivation for learning how to perform our own repairs is to save money. In the realm of auto repairs, it is always more economical to do it yourself, assuming, of course, that you know how to properly make the repair.

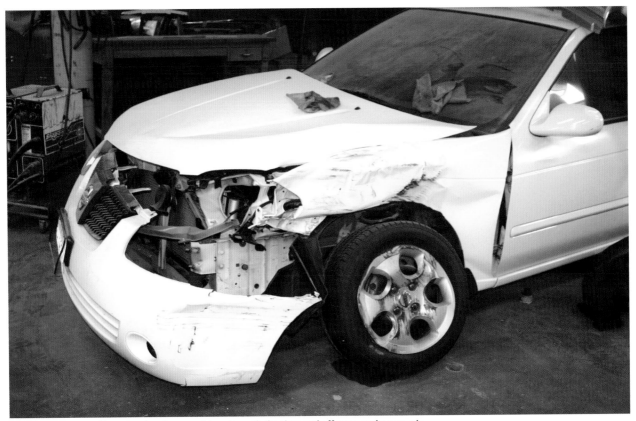
When newer cars suffer extensive damage, it is not worth the time and effort to make a repair.

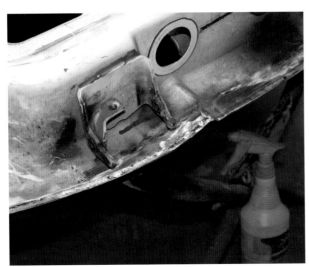
A simple door skin replacement can be installed in just hours by hammering over and spot welding the flange. This door panel has been brazed onto the door frame.

If you are going to do a repair on a quarter panel you will need to remove anything surrounding the area that will hinder access to the back portion of the quarter panel. While you are at it, start looking for additional problems, such as the rear hatch jamb damage.

You've heard it said that time is money, and in the repair business, time is big money. The labor rate of a body repair shop is an hourly figure that includes a flat-rate percentage (usually 40 or 50 percent) for the bodyman and the remaining 50 or 60 percent goes to the shop. So, in essence, whenever you have any kind of repair done at any shop, you are actually paying double for labor! That is why the total cost of a typical estimate is so astronomically high.

Cost is something that all of us have to take into account, and just about every decision that we are faced with when it comes to our cars boils down to the almighty dollar. I can't determine what you can or cannot afford, but what I can do is make you aware of the things that can cut into your budget. So the first thing to do when it comes down to making sensible choices concerning making a repair is to establish a budget. A budget must be realistic as well as flexible to a certain degree. The best way to come up with a good budget for your repair project is to do a little research.

To get your budget figure into the ballpark, the first step

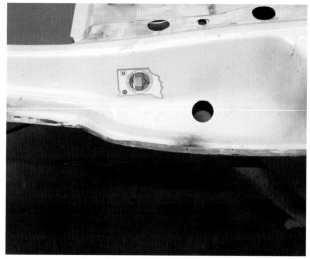

In many cases, a door skin can just be tack welded in a few places limiting the warpage by reducing the heat caused by welding.

A few Vise Grips will help keep a new door skin in place as you spot weld it on the frame.

Quite often, you will need to separate the door skin in the repair area and weld it back together after the repair of both the door skin and the door frame.

is to obtain a repair estimate from a local body shop. If you can get two or three estimates, that's even better. The more estimates that you can get with a breakdown of the itemized costs, the better and more accurate your budget will be. With a written itemized estimate in hand, you'll be able to immediately see how much money you stand to save by performing your own repair.

Knowing how a shop might estimate a job might give you some insight as to what you'd be paying for. First, many shops will charge you for an estimate, which involves carefully inspecting the vehicle for any unseen damage that is related to what appears to be a simple dent. Next, the shop will break down the labor hours involved to perform

the repair using a manual that provides recommended times for removing and replacing the parts involved. Depending on where the dent is located on the car, the shop might also allow for time to remove surrounding parts (i.e. inner panels, light assemblies, moldings, etc.) to access the damage. And then there is the actual repair time to fix the dent, which could range anywhere from two hours (the usual minimum regardless of how minor the damage is) to 16 or more hours for an extensively damaged panel.

Once the shop determines the labor cost, there are other items that are automatically added to the estimate to cover shop overhead, materials, consumables, and those annoying little incidentals that are unavoidable, such as disposal of

Many times damage is limited to a single door or fender. In the case of a door, start by removing the door so you can perform the repair off the vehicle.

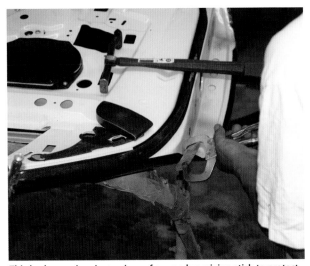

This body man is using a piece of a wooden mixing stick to protect the door skin flange from bending as the Vise Grip is utilized to hold the door skin in place.

Two new door skins and a professional job by the body man kept the repair cost to a minimum in this case. This job took about one day.

waste material. The estimated cost to repaint that fender is calculated in much the same way. And, although you are charged for the service of color matching the paint, you will always find a disclaimer in fine print stating that there is no guarantee of the color matching. We'll get into everything paint-related later on in the book.

For those who are fairly new to autobody repair, the decision of whether or not to replace a damaged panel should be determined by the job's learning value. While a particular job may be a little costlier, more difficult and

more time-consuming to repair, if you feel that you can expand your skills by doing it then give it a try.

A panel that may not look repairable often is. Just a hit here and a push there and it will be as good as new. Well,, there is a bit more involved than that. You do have to know where to hit it and how hard to hit it, but once you learn that, the rest is simple. When I was young and working in a body shop I worked in the back of the shop and the smart guys worked up front. I liked the back because it was less traveled and I could get more work done without interruptions, but the

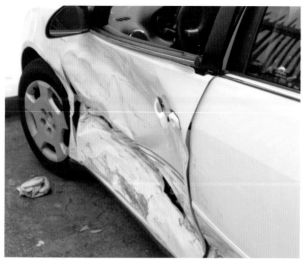

This side damage will require a bit more work than a door skin. It will require a new front fender and a rear quarter panel repair, but it is fixable. Most damaged cars will require a combination of repair and replacement of parts.

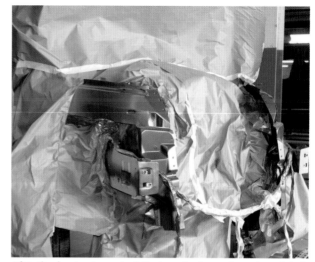

After the damage is repaired, the inner body panels can be painted, hiding any signs of the repair.

The dent in the fender is obvious and needed a repair, but the body man went one step further and repaired the dent under the bumper that would never have been seen. This is a very professional job.

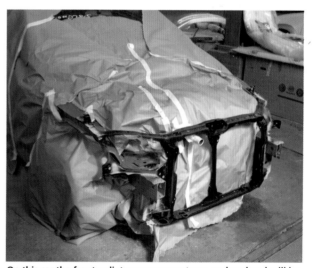

On this car the front radiator core support was replaced and will be painted to match the existing color, making it all but impossible to tell the car was ever damaged.

front was where the customers came in. And even though I thought it was a distraction, the guys working up front got the "gravy" jobs, while I got the ones no one else wanted. The junk filtered to the back of the shop, so I would end up with the worst and lowest-paying jobs, but I also got the oddball customers who wanted customizing treatments because they didn't have much money.

The bright side was that I learned how to repair the "unrepairable" and how to do it fairly fast, using my skill and imagination, not just bolting on new parts and taking home a nicer paycheck at the time. Most of the guys I worked with have since retired with little or no savings as I moved on to movie work and customizing, so the hard work and long hours did pay off and the term "save that fender" has come back to help me out as I have saved fenders on cars that were one-off or impossible to find parts for. In fact, the only time you will hear me say "throw that fender away" is if rust has ruined the fender first. Even then I may save it for a pattern… then throw it away.

New Panels

The skills required to replace or repair a body panel can vary depending on the panel and how it is attached to the car. Panels that are part of the main body, such as a quarter panel, will require an advanced level of skill to repair or replace. I do not recommend that you attempt to replace any panel that requires welding if you are a beginner. A bolt-on panel is any part of the car's body that is attached with fasteners and does not require welding. These usually include the left and right front fenders, front and rear valances, hood and decklid, and can be installed with a basic level of skill. Panels that are replaceable but are part of the main body include the left and right quarter panels (rear fenders), roof, cowl (the panel immediately below the windshield or rear window) and rocker panels. Most car doors, although bolt-on parts, are generally comprised of a door frame and skin, as well as all the hinge and latch hardware. They can be purchased as a complete assembly with the frame and outer skin welded from the factory,

"Keying" a car is the art of walking down the length of a car with your car keys against the side of the car costing the owner a few thousand dollars in repair and repaint costs. If the repair is not handled correctly, the scratch will keep showing up through the new paint job. I have seen shops replace the fenders and door skins, though this is an unnecessary expense. The best approach is to sand the scratch down to the metal and use a light coat of filler before repainting the area.

All these dents are easily repairable with simple body tools, as long as you know what you are doing. The front fender can be replaced or repaired, depending on the time and money involved.

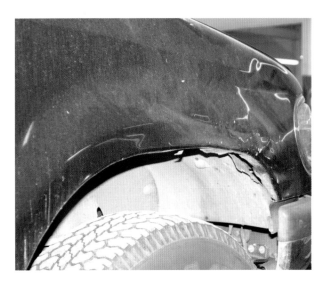

or you can purchase a door skin only. If the damage to a door has destroyed the outer skin, but left the inner frame structure intact, then you can save a substantial amount of money by replacing the outer skin and keeping the same inner frame.

Replacing a door skin is a fairly easy process. Most door skins are attached to the frame by a series of spot welds around the perimeter. Using a spot-weld drill, you can simply drill out each of the welds, pry the edge of the door skin away from the frame, and separate the two components. The new skin is installed by first carefully locating it on the existing frame, then bending the flanges into place around

the perimeter. You can either spot-weld along the flange for a factory appearance, or you can simply place intermittent tack welds along the edge with a MIG welder. The seam around the flange and the welds should then be protected with a sealer such as Evercoat's #365 Brushable Seam Sealer to prevent corrosion.

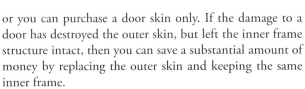

This type of job calls for a frame or body pull as the body is buckled under from the impact. This requires a piece of equipment most small shops do not own. This part of the repair is sometimes subcontracted out to a frame shop.

Body Panel ID

The level of difficulty to repair or replace body panels varies from model to model. Also, some cars may have additional body parts that are not identified in the accompanying illustration. Body panel replacement on most newer model vehicles requires minimal alignment, providing that the damage has not affected the main body. On older cars, the manufacturing tolerances were not as precise, and the need for shims and special alignment techniques are part of the job. Whether you have a '60s muscle car or a new import, the individual body panels are generally referred to by the following names:

- **HOOD:** Most late-model cars have a hood (or bonnet, as it's called across the pond) that extends from the base of the windshield to the front bumper cover, or fascia. In the interest of manufacturing and production efficiency, hood

designs have evolved over the years to eliminate the small cowl panel that spanned the base of the windshield on most pre-'80s vehicles.

- **COWL:** The late-model car in the illustration does not have a front or rear cowls panel, but the call-out shows you where they would be located. If you have a '60s or '70s muscle car, then chances are that you'll find a narrow panel with slotted vents along the base of the windshield. This front cowl is usually a bolt-on component and, due to its location under the windshield, is highly prone to rust damage. The rear cowl panel is located along the base of the rear window and is usually not a bolt-on. The rear cowl on certain General Motors cars of the '60s through '80s were highly rust prone due to the tendency of water to collect in the window trough. Unlike the front cowl, replacing the rear cowl requires window removal, cutting and welding.

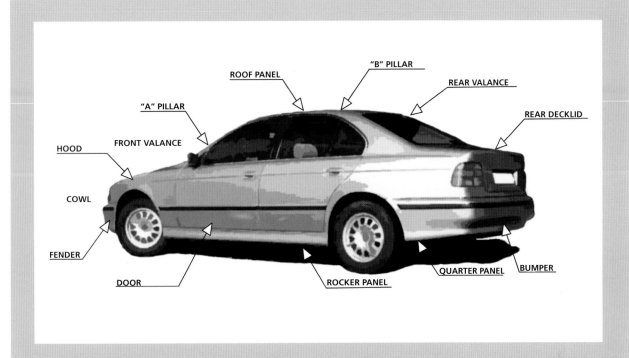

VALANCE: Sometimes called an apron, the valance is the panel located below the bumper that connects between the left and right front fenders. Some cars will have an upper valance or apron that also connects the left and right fenders, but is located immediately in front of the hood. The rear valance is located under the rear bumper and connects the left and right quarter panels. Valances are usually an easy bolt-on replacement.

FENDER: Most left and right front fenders extend from the leading edge of the doors to the front of the car, and most are bolt-on pieces. Depending on the extent of damage to a fender, you may or may not have to repair or replace the inner fender components such as the wheel well.

DOOR: All doors are bolted onto the main structure by way of hinges, however, they are not always considered easy bolt-on replacements. When a door is damaged, you might have to replace the whole door. However, if the damage is limited to the outer skin of the door and the door frame is unaffected, you can save money by "skinning" the door.

PILLAR: The pillars are structural posts that connect the roof panel to the main body. The "A" pillar is sometimes called the windshield post because it is narrow and usually part of the windshield frame. Hardtop sedans have at least two pillars (that is, two on the left and two on the right). Each pillar has a letter designation starting with "A" at the front. Some cars will have a "B" pillar post between the front and rear side windows, thus making the third pillar that connects the roof to the quarter panel the "C" pillar. Because the pillars are structural body components, they are not easily replaced. Seriously damaged pillars should be repaired by an experienced body repair person.

ROOF: A roof panel that is seriously damaged usually means that the vehicle has rolled over. A roll-over is definitely not a project for a weekend do-it-yourselfer! In the event of hail damage or some other surface dents, the roof panel is easier repaired than replaced.

QUARTER PANEL: Unlike the front fender, the rear fender, or quarter panel, is not a bolt-on body part. This is a structural part of the body that is welded and/or spot-welded into place by the factory. In order to replace a damaged quarter panel, you must justify both the cost and the amount of labor involved. In most cases, replacement of the quarter panel is best left to a professional.

Ever open your door, only to have it clipped by another car? This is not that uncommon and can be repaired with a new door skin and a bit of hammer and dolly work on the door frame. Or, you can replace the door with a quality used one if you can locate one at the local junkyard. The damage here was limited to the door only, other than a single chip in the fender paint.

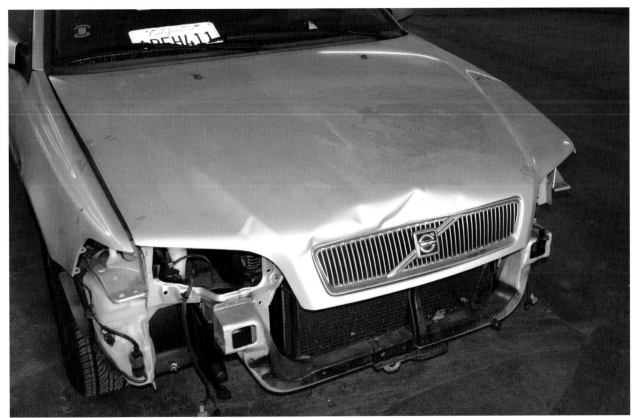

Since this is a Volvo, a new hood is going to be expensive. I would be very tempted to repair this one — after all, if it does not turn out right you can go ahead and buy a new one. At the very least, an attempt at a repair would be good practice.

Rear quarter panels are challenging to replace, so most people just try to repair them. A new panel means you'll need to worry about glass fitting, and removing and replacing the headliner.

New Used Panels

If a panel is damaged to the point of needing replacement and a new part is no longer available, you may have to scour the wrecking yards or log onto eBay to find a good used replacement. Keep in mind that purchasing used body parts, unlike new parts, is a buyer-beware deal, meaning that what you see is not always what you get. If you are purchasing a used body part that was previously part of another vehicle, be sure to inspect both sides of the panel for prior damage and for traces of rust. Don't assume that because a used part is smooth and painted that it is a good part.

Panel replacement can be as simple as taking the panel off and reversing the order to put the new one back on again. However the way you put the panel on makes a big difference. Just bolting it on is not enough. You have to align it perfectly first, which requires a bit of effort and a few shims and a knowledge of alignment. Getting a damaged vehicle to look as good or better than new requires more than smoothing out the body and laying on a perfect coat of paint. In order to achieve that show-quality look, each

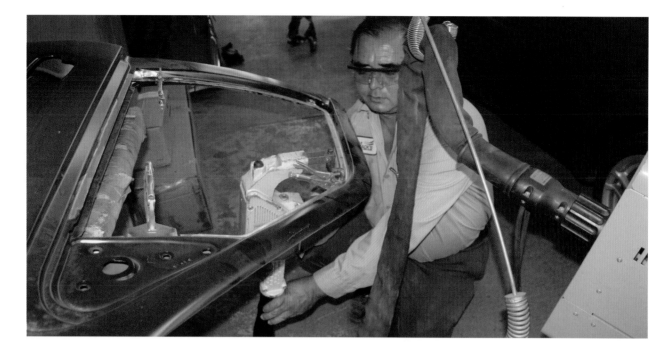

This new door skin is being spot welded onto the door frame with a portable spot welder. This is an expensive piece of equipment, but allows the correct method for fastening the door skin to the frame. The factories attach the skin the same way.

This DUZ-MOR repair system is used for pulling a body into correct alignment. Some shops specialize in this aspect of body/frame repairs and do not do the actual exterior fixes.

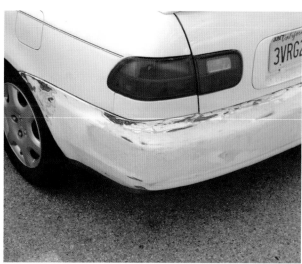

This is an example of what not to do! Bumpers on new cars are often made from urethane or other plastic and need to have special fillers used on them. This "backyard repair" will definitely not last.

This Discovery SUV allows a pretty straightforward rear quarter panel replacement. With the large flat panels of the body it would have been very hard to repair.

and every body seam, or gap, must be in perfect alignment. This means that reassembly plays as important a roll as the repair itself does.

We'll get into the details of reassembly and panel alignment in the next chapter.

Repair or Replace?

Chapter Six

Panel Alignment

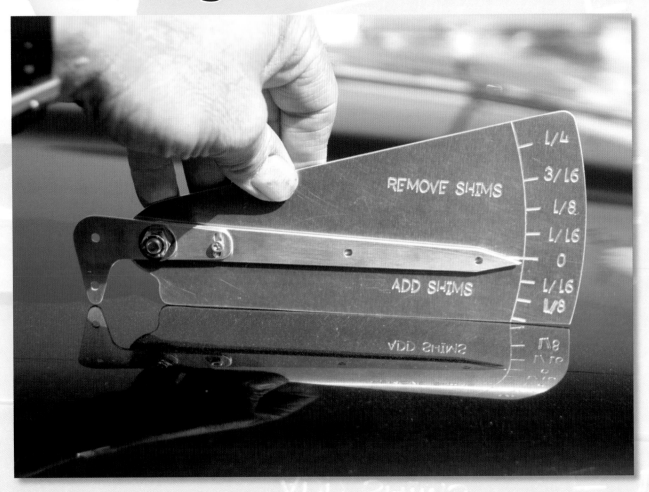

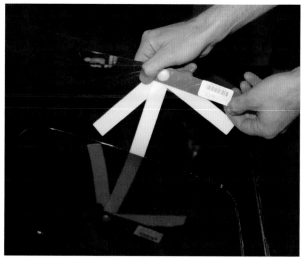

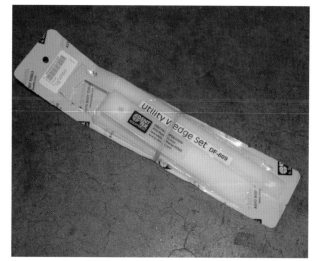

Eastwood sells a set of panel gap gauges that will allow you to check and adjust your door and panel gaps from 1/16 to up to about 1/4 inch. These gaps can be checked with about a plus or minus 1/32 accuracy. This set has eight blades.

Eastwood also sells a small pack of wedges for prying and lifting panels into alignment as you tighten the mounting bolts. This set also includes a plastic pry tool.

By stacking the wedges you can simply tap them in to raise a panel as you tighten the mounting screws.

Regardless of what type of vehicle you drive or how much of it you intend to repair, modify or restore, you shouldn't take it apart if you don't know how to put it back together. In this chapter, I'll cover some of the basic techniques and special tools that you can use to do just that including alignment of the hood, rear deck lid, and everything in between. If you watch a professional body repairman at work, you'll notice that he performs a lot of these procedures automatically whenever a panel is removed and replaced. There are tricks to getting everything lined up just right, and some handy devices in this chapter. These panel alignment devices are geared for the beginner as well as a serious do-it-yourselfer. They are easy to use, well made and relatively inexpensive.

If you've already tried your hand at replacing a panel on your car or truck, you may have discovered that some body parts require no trick at all to replace. Others, for instance a hood that was removed during an engine swap, can put even an experienced body man to the test, especially if the hinges were loosened or removed and no reference marks were made to indicate the original mounting position.

Panel alignment is critical and well worth learning. A door that is only 1/8 inch out of alignment may be difficult to latch or may not latch at all when closed. A hood that is 4 degrees out of square may hit the fender and chip the paint, or may jam shut, requiring cutting a hole in it just to open it.

Bad alignment is either due to poor assembly of the vehicle in the first place, or the result of some type of accident. However, it could be a result of a paint job where parts were removed for painting and not replaced correctly, or just not aligned at all after assembly.

When a car is involved in an accident, the damage oftentimes makes it impossible to simply replace a damaged panel with a new one. It's not uncommon to see a panel installed with a few of its bolts missing or an excessive amount of shims to compensate for a poorly repaired frame that doesn't measure up to spec. It doesn't take special training or expensive tools to align panels.

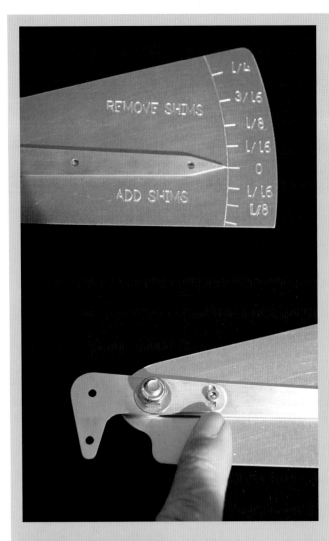

This little tool will tell you if a door or panel is misaligned within 1/64 inch and is simple to use and calibrate.

Nice Gaps!

A perfect or near-perfect seam on a car is not something that makes you stop and say, "Hey buddy, nice door gaps!" But if the alignment is off, the seams become very noticeable, especially if the car is painted with a light color. As you become more familiar with this aspect of auto bodywork, you'll soon develop a discerning eye for body details. A few hours can make the difference between a pristine-looking car and a mediocre car. Panel alignment is an art and is more confusing than it is difficult. It requires a few inexpensive tools and a few hours, but can make a difference of thousands of dollars in the end value of your car.

If you've noticed that your car has misaligned panels, there are a few preliminary checks to perform before you start. As with any mechanical problem, an accurate pinpoint diagnosis is a must in order for your repair efforts to be effective. Obviously, if misaligned panels have appeared after a collision, it's fairly simple to determine where the problem is. But, if misalignment is something that you've noticed gradually over a period of time, then a little investigation is in order. In most cases, a panel drops out of alignment for a reason and the misalignment is merely a symptom of the problem, not the problem itself. Some of the more obvious areas to look for the source of uneven gaps and panel misalignment are the body or frame for previous damage, worn or improper fastening hardware, loose bolts, bent or missing brackets and worn-out hinges.

Normally, I shy away from making blatant endorsements for products that my company manufactures, but I have to make an exception here. For those of you who are having problems with aligning any part of your vehicle's body, I

This pry bar is good for moving panels without scraping the paint on finished panels.

This tool just attaches to most floor jacks and replaces the front lift plate.

The E-Z-rest can hold and lift the door into proper alignment as you re-attach it to the car, turning a two-person job into a one-person task.

highly recommend that you check out my How-To Series DVDs and videos. We've recently released a segment on panel alignment that covers everything from troubleshooting, to tools, to techniques. All of my DVDs and videos are available from www. epindustries.com, or you can purchase them from The Eastwood Company at www.eastwoodco.com. Some other handy tools for this type of work are:

- **Panel gap gauge** (31129) for checking and adjusting the gap in doors or panels to the same gap, this is a set of spacers that allow you to stack shims to what ever thickness you need up to about .445 inch, which is much more than you will ever need.
- **The utility wedge** set DF-609 includes a few wedges and a plastic non-marring prybar.
- **E-Z Rest door hanger** allows you to hang a door by yourself. It is padded to prevent marring

and will cradle the door, allowing you to bolt the hinges in place. It replaces the round plate on the end of a standard floor jack.

- **The panel alignment gauge** will detect as little as a 1/64-inch difference in panel height. It is simple to use and will hold the readout when you remove the gauge.
- **Soft automotive tools.** The Auto-Tool is used on automotive interior and exterior moldings. These tools are used in the production of Toyota and Lexus vehicles. The Auto-Tool is sturdy and will not scratch most plastics. The Auto-Tool is ideal for other automotive applications, such as stereo/alarm installation, glass and body shop applications.
- **The door alignment tool** adjusts sagging doors so they close properly.

The door strike can be adjusted by loosening it and re-tightening it in a new position.

The bear claw locking mechanism is slightly adjustable — it can be moved about 1/4 inch in all directions.

Panel Alignment

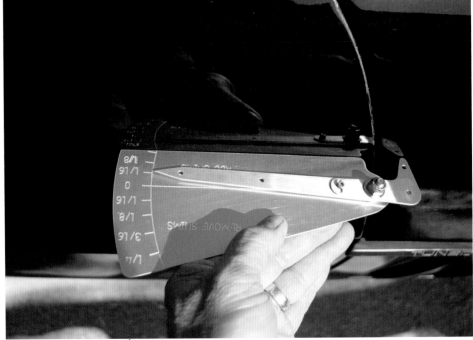

This is a handy little gauge I came up with that allows you to not only detect an out-of-alignment panel, but it will tell you how many shims to add or subtract to the adjoining panel to bring it into proper alignment.

Tips for Perfect Alignment

➤ NEVER put a car on jack stands during the process of body alignment. This will warp the car, as all cars are designed to sit on the tires and be supported by the suspension points of the frame and nowhere else. The simple "jacking up" of a car by a side frame rail can tweak the body to the point that it is no longer possible to open the door. A car can twist as much as two inches by jacking the car from a corner of the frame.

➤ Most hinges and mounting brackets are designed to set up for shimming to achieve perfect alignment. I knew a guy that worked for Rolls-Royce that used very thin sheet

Door hinges are normally bolted in and can be either adjusted or shimmed into proper alignment by simply loosening the bolts and slipping a shim under the hinge base and re-tightening the bolt.

Most door strikes can be adjusted by loosening the two, three or even four screws that hold them in place and moving the striker. The screws on this striker are hidden by a plastic cover.

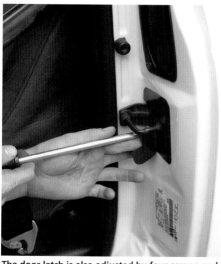

The door latch is also adjusted by four screws and should be moved a little at a time to avoid jamming the door into the body.

On this old Mustang, the door striker is adjusted by two screws. When the striker is badly worn, it's best to just replace it, or you will probably be battling alignment problems.

metal shims to get "perfect alignment" of body parts. A trick I used to use to align hoods, doors and deck lids was to loosen the attachment bolts slightly, then lightly close the door, hood or deck. I then pushed or pried (with plastic tools) the panel or door into perfect alignment, then carefully opened the door, hood or deck and tightened the bolts. In many cases, this is enough of take care of the alignment.

This little tool was invented just as this book was written and is a tool that will aid in the alignment process as well as indicate to the operator how far out of alignment a panel or door actually is. A 1/16 alignment mistake can be surprisingly hard to spot with the naked eye. This little tool will show you not only the difference in height between two panels, but also how much of a shim you need to add or subtract to bring the panel within limits. It is simple to use and needs no calibration.

Doors are simple to align if you have the right

While not an alignment issue, this spring on many cars is required to keep the door open and will need to be installed if it's missing. On many cars it is located on the bottom hinge.

Panel Alignment

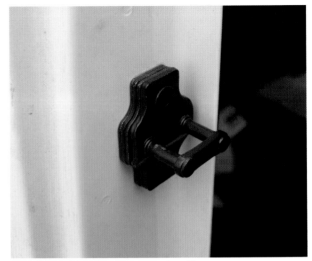

This striker has been shimmed so it can reach the latch. This was required at the factory because of improper door fit.

New low-cost cars now have hinges welded in place, making it impossible to adjust the door unless you bend the mounting plates in the door jamb. This is not recommended.

tools and enough knowledge to use them. A door hanger is a great tool if you are working alone and need an extra hand.

➤ This simple tool attaches to your floor jack and allows the weight of the door to be carried by the floor jack. You simply pull out your jack plate and slip this into the opening left over from the jack plate pin. Then you slide this tool under your door and gently jack the door up, relieving the weight of the door only. Be careful you don't

lift too much or the door will be pushed out of alignment as soon as the bolts are loosened. There is a fine line between too much and too little, but it is better to have too little pressure on the bottom of the door than too much. Error on the side of caution. Once the door bolts are loose you can jack the door up a little more, bringing it into proper alignment.

➤ Never loosen all of the hinge bolts at once when aligning a door — leave one snug, but not tight. This will allow some degree of movement without the door flopping all around. You should not need to remove hinges from the cowl unless the door is badly out of alignment.

➤ Door alignment can be frustrating and will task you nerves, so take it one step at a time. Think in single directions and movements at a time, such as first bringing the door flush at the hinge area at the upper part of the door, then the lower hinge area.

➤ If the door fits well but is not far enough forward. NEVER loosen top and bottom hinges and move it forward. Loosen the top hinge to the cowl/center post and lift the rear of the door, a LITTLE. This will push the upper hinge forward. Then TIGHTEN that one bolt that was left snug. Do the same on the lower hinge, pushing down, but remember, the weight of the door is helping, so little push is needed.

➤ If the door fits well but is out at the top or the bottom, again, loosen ONE hinge and push it out or in. If it is out or in at the top rear, for instance, move the bottom front in the opposite direction. This will pivot the door on the striker and move the rear top where you want. Moving the bottom rear requires moving the top front.

➤ You may need to twist the door. If the front fits well and rear is out at the top, you can put a block of wood at the rear of the door at the top and push in on the bottom to twist the door. Some will take a lot of force to bend, so be very careful not to let your fingers hang around the outside of the door edge.

➤ If you are hanging the door and you have access to the hinges (either through the wheel well with the skirt off

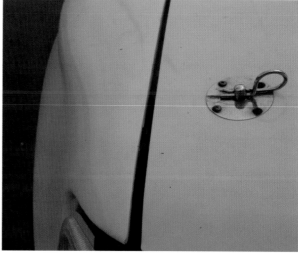

In this case, the hood pins are pulling the hood to one side, so moving them would pull the hood back into perfect alignment. This is a simple repair, but a common mistake.

Hood hinges are a bit more complicated as they will allow you to move the hood forward and rearward as well as sideways. With a few shims the hood can be lifted, if it is sitting too low.

or if the fender itself is off) you can simply hold the door up to the opening and push the latch shut. Then put the bolts in the hinge.

◄ Hoods are a special case for alignment as they are a large sheet of shaped metal or fiberglass that is suspended at its longest end. This puts a lot of stress in the hood panel itself, as the hinges are spring loaded in most cases to allow the hood to stay open. This pre-stressed hinge wants to buckle the hood in the center, so to keep this from happening you have to be sure that the hood hinges are will lubricated and free to "hinge." Old Chevy trucks are famous for this "center hood buckling," and to make matters worse the hood is weak at the mid-point by design. So check the center return on the hood for cracks or tears in the metal or cracks in the fiberglass before an alignment continues. If no damage is found, or it is found and repaired, you can continue with the alignment.

◄ The best place to start on hood alignment is to first remove the hood latch mechanism to prevent the hood from locking. Once the hood is in alignment the latch can be replaced and aligned separately from the basic hood alignment. Even the hood latch can pull the hood out of alignment, so care must be taken when aligning this as well.

◄ When replacing the hood latch, use a piece of clay or something similar and put it on the latch. This way you can see exactly where it hits when you do install the latch. Bring the hood down until you just tap the clay, but DON'T LATCH IT. This tells you where you have to move the latch.

◄ If you have a hood where the hinge mounts on the side of the fender or the side of the cowl like with an older car or truck, you'll want to "rotate" the hinge on the fender. Just pushing the hinge up and down will give you very little movement on the top of the hood.

◄ Something to keep in mind when aligning your hood: if you raise the back of the hood on the hinge, or raise the back of the hinge on the fender, the hood will go

This hood is setting too high on the passenger side and only took about 10 seconds to bring into proper alignment without even using a tool; we simply turned the hood stops down, allowing the hood to sit lower on this side. The two hood stops are located on top of the radiator core support.

We make a tool that allows you to check for proper alignment of a panel and also know how thick of a shim to add or subtract.

Using a plastic wedge and a hammer, you can often tap a hood into proper alignment without damaging the paint.

Hoods are held in place by adjustable latches on the body and an adjustable striker on the hood. Hood alignments sometimes require loosening the latch slightly, closing the hood gently, moving everything into proper alignment, then re-tightening the latch. It can get a little tricky, so be careful and have patience.

Poor body part alignment can lower the value of a truck or car and is often an indicator of low cost after-market parts. But with a little care and skill even these parts can be brought back into proper alignment.

On a recent job for Disney/Pixar, we had to build Mater, and even though the truck had to look rundown and ragged, some seams needed to be invisible. Less-than-perfect alignment was unacceptable.

up. Something to keep in mind when aligning your hood is that, if your raise the back of the hood on the hinge or raise the back of the hinge on th fender, the rear of the hood will be raised and the whole hood will go up. If you raise the "front" of the hood on the hinges or the front of the hinge on the fender, the whole hood will be lowered. The best way to learn this is to play with a hood and try adjusting the hood hinge by adding and removing shims until you understand hinge-to-hood relationships. You have to remember you are working with a pivot point in the hinge, not a stationary part. So if you loosen the FRONT bolt on the hood (where it bolts to the hinge) and put a shim or washer between the hood and hinge, this will LOWER the hood on that side. If you put that same washer under the rear bolt it will RAISE the rear of the hood on that side. Now, if you loosen the bolts from the hinge to fender and close the hood, the hinge will rotate on down in the front right? This will raise the REAR of the hood the same as putting a shim in the back bolt between the hinge and hood.

➤ **To lower the back the hood**, loosen the bolts (only slightly) and PUSH UP on the front of the hood. This rotates the hinges back, thus raising the front of the hinge and lowering the hood in the back.

➤ Always leave one bolt snug on the hinge. If you want to rotate it back, leave the front bolt tight. If you want to rotate it forward, leave the rear bolt tight. When you move the hood forward or back on the hinge, leave the bolts snug enough that you have to tap on the edge of the hood to get it to move. Or if it needs to go back, leave the bolts a little snug and wiggle the hood up and down. The weight of the hood will make it slide down. Remember, it only needs a 1/16-inch or so to make a 3/16 inch or more change at the front. To pull the hood forward on the hinge loosen them so they are still a little snug so you have to pull up on the back of the hood to make it slide that little bit. If you loosen it up so it moves anywhere you want it, you'll never know how much you moved it and you'll probably move it too much.

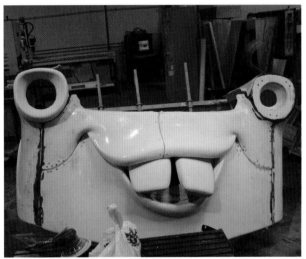

The front end of Mater, which we fabricated from 1/4-inch ABS over wooden plugs, was prepared from many small parts, which were aligned and fitted to match perfectly. Everything was then bonded with a special adhesive.

➤ Get the hood laying flat first, then move the hood forward or back on each side to make the hood fit the hole between the fenders.

➤ You may need to move fenders as well. Just do each change slowly, move it a very small amount each time. Look at the bolt and washer as you move the panel; you will see where the washer used to be, the amount is much easier to control if you watch the washer movement.

➤ **If you need to move the hood up or down at the front**, there are a few ways to do it. First, on each side there are the "bumpers." The hood bumpers are located at each front corner and look like bolts with rubber pads on top. Just unlock the jamb nut and raise or lower the "bolt" so it holds the hood at the height you need to match the fender. You may find that the hood won't go low enough even with the bumper down far enough. The latch may not be down far enough. When you close the hood, you shouldn't be able to pull up on the hood or push it down.

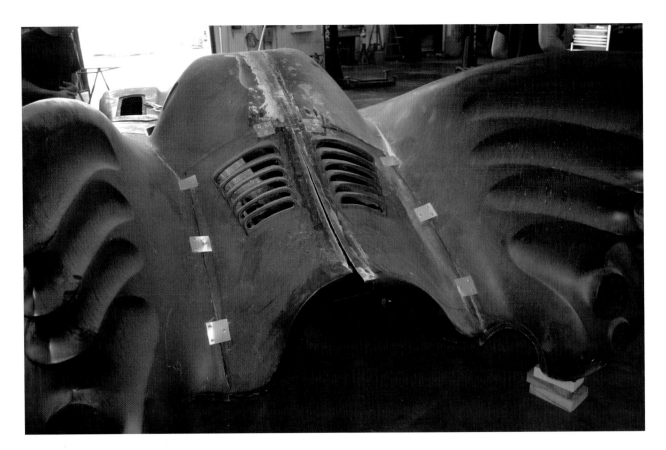

On this kit car a customer had us work on, the seams were wide, narrow and out of alignment all at the same time. All we could do was add what we call "tangs" to bring the body back into relative alignment and then have the seams re-glassed so we could cut new seams. The "tangs" are round sections of sheet metal or aluminum with small 3/16-inch holes drilled in them so you can pop rivet them to the body, helping you align the body as you go along. This system will at least make sure the body is on the same plane.

The latch should be tight enough to hold it against the bumpers tight, but not too tight. If you have to apply too much force to open the hood or it opens with a loud "pop," the latch is probably too tight. If it is at the right height but you can lift it up some, then the latch needs to be moved down.

◄ **Aligning the trunk lid** is similar to adjusting the hood, except that the hinges do not normally move. Therefore, your only options beyond the movement in the slotted holes are shimming and twisting. If that's still not

enough, then your only option may be to bend the hinge or the quarters. We recommend that you only do this if you have exhausted every other possibility.

Panels

◄ Most of the tips for doors and the hood work on panels, with a few differences. Start with fitting the rear top of a fender. I like to put all the bolts in loose enough so the fender can easily move. Close the door, and with the hood open adjust the gap at the top of the rear of the

Cars made from metal are a bit harder to work on than fiberglass or ABS, but the same principles apply: Align every panel with the next one. Each panel will affect the next, so an overall approach is required.

fender to door. After you tighten other bolts, this cannot be modified, so do it first. Tighten the bolt under the hood closest to the door to secure the position. You may need to shim a bolt to move the fender forward or back. After you have that bolt tight and the gap is to your liking, open the door and tighten the rear fender bolt that is at the top of the fender in the door jamb. Then do the bottom bolt. With the door closed, adjust your gap. You may need to wedge a flat blade screwdriver or body spoon to "force" the fender forward to get the desired gap. Or just the opposite — use a 2 x 4 or something similar off the front tire to force the fender back to get the gap. This is one of the hard spots to get perfect because you have to get both the gap and the in-and-out of the fender to door at the same time with the same bolt. Or just the opposite, use a length of 2 x 4 or something similar with the end perched on the front tire of the car to force the fender backwards to close the fender-to-door gap slightly. This is one of the hardest spots to adjust properly because you have to get both the gap correct and align the fender plane to the door plane at the same time, holding them in proper alignment with the same bolt.

▶ Bending a panel or adjacent panel is sometimes required. You can get this done in a number of ways; one is to use a block of wood. For example, let's say that along the edge of the hood there is a spot that is high, but the front and the rear are perfect. You can lay a block of wood on the spot, right at the edge where it is strong. Using a big hammer (the bigger the better, trying to make a small hammer do the job can cause a lot of damage) hold the block and strike it nice and solid. Then check the results, you may need many strikes to do it. In doing this you may

want to support the hood at the front with a block of wood under the hood. This way the hood is up off the fender and it will bend easier because of the solid rest it has. You can also put the block under the edge of the hood at a low spot and with steady pressure bend it down at a point.

▶ If you are working with very tight tolerances, you can actually grind the edge of a panel or jamb to get an extra fraction of an inch. Be very careful and use a fine disk like 80- or 120-grit. Take a LITTLE off. You don't want to grind the metal thin, of course, but a little can make a big difference when you are fighting for fractions. You really won't be cutting too much metal, you are really just cleaning off ALL the primer and paint there. Then when you prime it, don't put a lot or sand it thin so there will be very little on the edge.

▶ Shims are just spacers that can be used to bring a panel, hood or trunk into proper alignment usually after body damage. At one time, shims were used by the factory to compensate for loose tolerances straight off the production line. There are a number of types and styles and thicknesses, Body shims have a slotted hole so you can add the shim just by loosening the body bolt and not have to remove the bolt altogether. Shims are cheap and it's best to have a small supply of them on hand.

Panel Alignment

Chapter Seven

Rust Repair and Treatment

This 1972 Mustang fastback shows how rust can help reduce a car from an $80,000 classic to a $2,500 project.

One of the biggest factors that might determine whether to fix a damaged panel or to replace it is rust, also known as corrosion or body rot. In order for rust to occur, three elements must be combined. The first is iron, or steel, which is what most car bodies are constructed of. The second is oxygen, which constitutes approximately 21 percent of the air that we breathe. The third is water, which also contains a percentage of oxygen. Chemical compounds such as salt (as in seawater), and those found in acid rain only serve to enhance the electrolyte qualities of water, thereby promoting rust.

Rust begins to develop as soon as water contacts a bare iron or a steel surface, although you may not actually see the brownish-colored corrosion appear that soon. The water, being an adequate electrolyte (a liquid that allows electron movement), combines with carbon dioxide in the atmosphere to create a type of mild acid, which is an even better electrolyte than plain water. As this mild acid forms on a bare metal surface, the iron elements begin to dissolve. The individual components of water (hydrogen and oxygen) tend to separate and the oxygen bonds with the dissolved iron to form iron oxide, or rust.

You might be asking yourself, "How does a car that rolls off the dealer lot with a nice protective coat of paint on it start to rust?" Well, if you look closely at car bodies that show signs of rust, you'll more than likely see what appears to be a bubbling of the paint. In fact, it takes quite a while for the brown-colored corrosion to actually break through, but once it does, it's a sure sign that rust has been eating away at the metal for quite a long time.

A rusted-out rocker panel had a "patch panel" fabricated and welded in.

Since rust begins to appear as bubbles in the finish, this should tell you that the process of corrosion begins either underneath the layer of paint, or on the back side of the panel where a section of bare metal might have been exposed. A cured layer of automotive paint serves as a waterproof barrier from the elements, so the only place for water to contact the panel is on the backside where paint coverage is minimal, or through a previously repaired spot that wasn't properly treated.

One area on a car where rust is usually very prevalent is the rocker panels. Not only are the rockers located at the lowest point, but they also form a gutter-like trough along the body

Rust will start wherever water gets trapped and held for any length of time, such as behind the chrome in the body seam, or in the bottom of a door panel, if the panel is not designed with a good drain system. This '40 Ford apparently had a lot of these areas.

After a lot of work, I finally had the rust removed and the body ground down to metal.

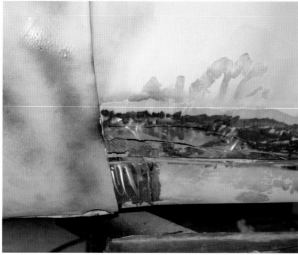

Patch panels were added to the *Cobra* Merc during its restoration. This works well, but the rust will re-appear eventually if the panel still traps water.

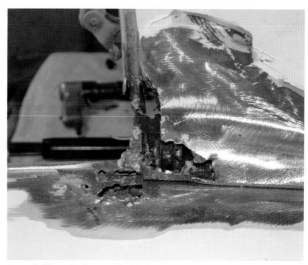

Some brilliant body man decided to repair this trunk by stuffing holes with newspaper and body filler.

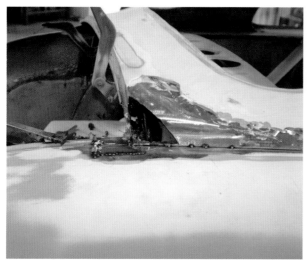

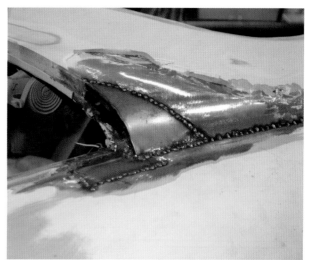

We ground the area down to metal and replaced the bad area with new metal. It probably took less time than the former repair did.

where moisture can accumulate. And since the inner surfaces of the rockers are not exposed to the paint application, the bare metal begins to rust through from the inside out.

Damage Assessment

When considering repair work on rusted panels, you must first evaluate the extent of the rust. This can be done with a simple visual inspection of the rust-damaged metal. If you see what appears to be a patch of blistering or bubbling of paint, this is a telltale sign that rust has corroded into the metal. If you've made the decision to dig in and make the repair, the first step is to chip away the blistered paint to see how bad the rust is. In most cases, regardless of how small the blistered area is, there will be a point where the corrosion has completely penetrated the sheet metal. There are several tools that you can use to initiate this step of the job.

The way we approach rust that has blistered the paint is to start off by grinding away the blister and a small area around it. We use a small pneumatic right-angle grinder

such as a Chicago Pneumatic CP875 with a 2- or 3-inch Roloc backing pad fitted with a 36-grit disc. (Refer to the accompanying photos for a step-by-step look at rust repair techniques.) Removing the top coats of paint, sealer and primer makes it possible to inspect the area to determine the extent of the rust. What you will most likely see after taking down the blistered spot with the grinder is rusty metal that has begun to pit and spread. To a certain extent, this can be repaired without patching or replacing the entire panel, especially if the area is small.

If a bolt-on panel, such as a fender or valance, is infected with rust and a replacement is affordable and available, consider replacing the panel but keeping the rusted original piece to practice your work on. The lower valance (front or rear) and even the left or right front fender are easy to remove and replace, and usually are the least expensive parts of the body that you can buy. If the repair to the original part is successful, you'll have a spare to save or to sell.

Small rust spots as described above, even if they appear in numerous areas along the bottom of a car, fall under

I recently purchased a 1940 Ford four-door that was sold to me on eBay as a "restorable" car. Well, it wasn't, but it did make a great subject for rust repair and a good basis for a custom car that I wanted to build, so all was not lost.

Once I pulled the carpet up I found the ground staring up at me through what used to be the floorboards.

the "minor rust" category. If the metal is not rusted all the way through, I prefer to repair almost everything that is damaged. And if the car is old or a little rare or unusual, you'll need to repair it because the replacement parts may not exist. Another factor to consider is that it may take you more time to find a part may than it takes to repair a damaged or rusted part.

I enjoy fixing a panel that somebody says cannot be repaired and making it all but impossible to see the repair, even from the backside. It can be very rewarding and

actually save you money if you can spend the time repairing the panel once you learn how to do it. But there are times when you have to replace a panel, and one of those times is when rust has completely taken over. If this is the case then make sure you know what you are getting. There have been a few times that I have bought panels over the Web, only find out that they were in worse shape than the piece I was replacing.

I live and California and have most of my life, and rust is something I associate with the East Coast (except right

Bruce started removing what was left of the original sheet metal. The frame was also a bit rusty.

Paper has more structural integrity than this floor had. The floor needed to be replaced with new metal.

After all the metal (rust) was removed, I laid down some stiff poster board and started tracing around the frame. This would be my pattern for a new set of floorboards.

along the Pacific Ocean, there we get rust!). In any event, I used to buy cars at auctions every so often and from a private party occasionally if the deal sounded good. Well, one crisp autumn morning as the sun was just creeping across the front of my shop I received a phone call from a guy who wanted $500 for a 1995 Toyota truck. The year was 1996 and I thought that was an unbelievable price for a Toyota. Even at twice that price would have been great. He stated that he needed the money fast and in cash and

asked if I would buy the truck if he showed up at my shop with it. I told him that I was more than a bit suspicious and had a few questions before I would commit to a truck that I had not seen. His response was "fire away" to which I did. The conversation went somewhat as follows:

EP *Is it legal? I do not buy hot cars!*
Deep Throat: *Yes, in fact I have the pink slip in my hand!*

You cannot "fit" a template enough times because you will always find something to trim or add on to an area. I do this by simply taping a section of cardboard on top of the template and re-trimming it to fit.

Using a shop knife, I cut on the line that was marked on the "foam core," trimming it down to the required size for the main template.

I added the front sections on by using different pieces of cardboard to extend the first piece. This is a much easier method than starting with one large piece of cardboard and trimming it to fit. These were simply duct taped in place.

EP: *Has it been wrecked, flipped over or totaled in any way?*

Deep Throat: *Not a dent in the truck!*

EP: *How about the engine, is it knocking or leaking oil?*

Deep Throat: *Not a drop, and the engine only has about 40,000 miles on it!*

EP: *Well then how about the interior, is it missing?*

Deep Throat: *No, it is all there…do you want it or not?*

EP: *Sure, bring it down, I'll buy it!*

Deep Throat: *Now, if I do bring it to you, you will buy it, for sure?*

I told him I would, and he showed up about 30 minutes later. Once I walked out in the driveway and saw the truck I felt like a fool. I forgot to ask him about rust! The truck was so rusted that I could see the engine and him inside the truck without opening the hood or doors. It was amazing that he made it to the shop. But to his credit, it did run and

I often draw a pattern on our AutoCad system, then print it out and use it for reference during the layout stage of the pattern-making process.

Using a good set of sheet metal sheers makes cutting sheet metal easy. Just learn to stay on the line — or learn to weld better as you put the metal back on the section you inadvertently cut off.

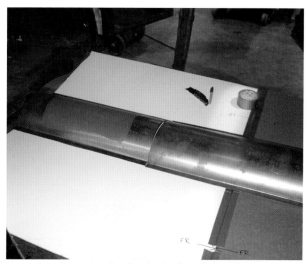

I sometimes jump ahead and make the driveshaft well just to have it as a reference during the pattern making process. The well is made out of two pieces instead of one because my "roll machine" is only a 4-foot roll and I can't fit a full driveshaft well into it.

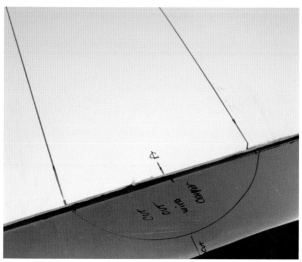

Next, I marked the rear vertical section that will give the bottom panel a bit more strength when it is bent upwards. The radius cut is for the driveshaft well.

The main pattern, now cut from metal, is laid out on a metal table to start the shaping and welding process.

Shaping of the floorboards starts with the rear section being bent up at 90 degrees.

As seen from the front, the rear section is taking shape.

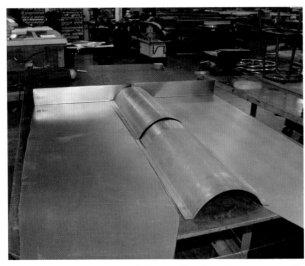

The center well is in place and the new floorboard is coming together. This is the best time to trim any areas that are overlapping or not fitting correctly. It is much more difficult to trim everything after the pieces have been welded.

Next I make a series of small tack welds, keeping the heat to a minimum as I move around the panels.

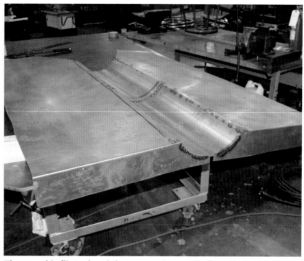

The panel is flipped and the process is repeated on the bottom.

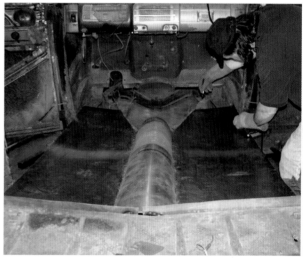

The floor is fitted again as a few things have changed. The driveshaft well has a tendency to widen the whole floorboard, requiring a bit more trimming.

I mark the areas that need more trimming.

I ground away the area where the new floorboard will be welded and finally hit good solid metal.

The front two floor panels were cut, bent and added. They would later be welded onto the main panel after alignment.

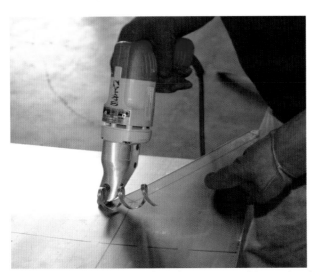

The transmission well is cut out from the same gauge (18 gauge) as the floor and rolled to match the required curve.

he was correct on all the points that I asked him about, so I bought it off him, more for a joke than anything else. We eventually used it as a movie prop. Subsequently, I received a return on my investment and he sold his rust bucket before it fell apart on the highway. But this taught me to include the question, "Does it have any rust?" in my future inquiry to a person selling me a car.

Depending on the extent of the problem, you can either grind rust down or replace the panel. That decision is totally dependant on the severity of the rust and how far it has propagated across the metal.

The repair could be as simple grinding and filling the area

with a metal treatment to slow the rust down. I say "slow the rust down" because once started, rust will continuously eat and destroy metal and, unless you properly treat it, corrosion will eventually spread to every part of your car. You cannot reverse the process of rust, even though many products claim to. In fact, you can't really ever stop it (according to the second law of thermodynamics), but you can slow it down to the point that, for all intents and purposes, it has stopped. Many of the chemicals that we use to slow rust down are good, but in the long run you may need to perform a bit of minor surgery, or even major surgery.

The edges are bent up and the part placed for final fit or trimming.

A few taps with a soft blow hammer and the well fits perfectly.

The top piece is added after it is cut, shaped and bent, leaving a gap for the last piece of metal that will finish off the front of the floorboard.

A sturdy new floor is taking shape.

A piece of tracing paper is good for getting the shape needed to fill a gap. The pattern can later be transferred to a piece of metal for the final front piece.

Patch Panels

Spot panel replacement is a pretty simple procedure, and replacing a fender or door will not take long, either. But the rusted area where most people draw the line and say, "I won't go there!" are the floorboards. Actually, the floor can be the simplest panel of all to replace. If you're lucky, you might find a set of reproduction sheet metal floor pans, but more than likely, the biggest problems you'll come across there will be cost and availability. The cost of some repro parts nowadays requires getting a second mortgage on your garage.

The better way to go, of course, is to make it yourself. You can buy the metal and all the tools to do it in a weekend for less than the cost of buying the floor from an Internet site and having it shipped to you. And when you're done, it will be what you want, not what you get. If you want to build a stronger floor, you can simply use thicker metal. If you want to lower the seats, you can build dropped pans in the seat area. It is all up to you. And yes, it's really that simple!

A project like this can intimidate most people. There is a trick involved, somewhat like there is with mountain climbing: "Don't look down!" When replacing the

I start the welding with the areas that are in alignment, making the unit a one-piece floorboard and adding a lot of strength by the design of the parts. I will later add some square tubing under some areas after testing it for loads.

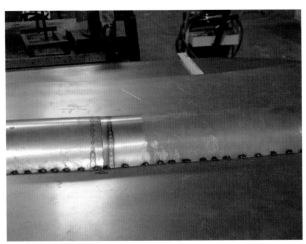

floorboards, looking at the project overall will scare the heck out of you. Just focus on a single area at a time and replace that one small area, then move on to the next spot and repair that area. Before you know it, the whole floor will be replaced. Whenever I take on a project like this, I often look back when it's completed, and realized that if I looked at it in its entirety I would have never tackled the project and assumed it "almost impossible." It's far better to break your project down into bite-size chunks so they're easily digestible. Then you can take on the biggest of projects, even that rusty old floorboard. Or, if the rust has settled in a door or fender, you may want to start with the fabrication of a patch panel that you build yourself from a flat piece of body metal and shape to fit snuggly into the offending area.

Eddie Paul's *Paint & Bodywork Handbook*

A section of square tubing added a lot of strength at the rear vertical plate. The floorboard is now ready to add to the car, once the frame is finished.

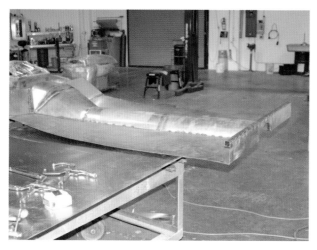

This may require a simple cutting and fitting of a small piece of metal, or more advanced shaping with an English wheel, planishing hammer and a shrinker-stretcher. In the long run, however, you'll be glad you did it yourself.

Making a patch panel may sound scary, but it really isn't if broken down into small steps. The first step in rust is simply to find out how bad the rust is. When looking for rust on body panels, make sure to look on both sides. If your are searching for rust is under the carpet you will need to at least poke the carpet with a sharp pinch or "awl" to see if it pokes through the floor boards. You may want to pull the carpet and visually check for rust.

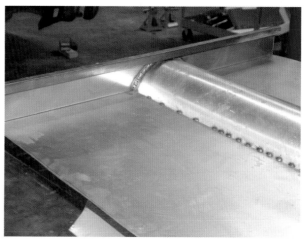

Rust treatment chemicals from left to right: Eastwood Oxisolv is a rust removing gel that leaves a zinc phosphate coating on the metal surface. POR-15's Metal Ready is a phosphoric acid/zinc phosphate solution that follows the application of POR-15 Marine Clean Industrial Strength Cleaner and Degreaser. Good old Naval Jelly Rust Dissolver from Loctite is a reliable and easy-to-use treatment that has been around for many years.

Chemicals of Rust Repair

Repairing, or more accurately, removing rust on automotive body panels involves special techniques, as well as special chemicals. The most popular method of rust removal that does not involve the use of chemicals is sandblasting. Sandblasting is performed with equipment ranging from an inexpensive hand-held blaster to a full-size industrial enclosure. For spot blasting small areas of rust, a hand-held tool works well. You can purchase special blasting media (i.e. sand) from supply houses such as Eastwood, or you can run down to your local Home Depot and pick up a bag of white playground sand. The grit size of the sandbox sand is ideal for automotive purposes. If you plan to use a portable sandblaster, be sure to glove up and wear adequate face protection as the blasting particles tend to ricochet off the metal.

The chemicals of rust repair include products such as the old standby, Naval Jelly, rust dissolver, and a number of metal etching solutions, which are mild (diluted) mixtures of phosphoric acid or muriatic/hydrochloric acid and water. Por-15's Metal Ready is a phosphoric solution that works well and is easy to use. The metal should be de-scaled and cleaned first with the Por-15 Marine Clean cleaning solution. As always, follow the manufacturer's instructions and be sure to wear the proper protective gear. Safety goggles will keep splashing fluids out of your eyes and neoprene gloves will prevent chemical burning of your skin. Another thing to remember when etching metal with an acid solution is to neutralize the acid residue with a baking soda wash and rinse the treated area thoroughly with water.

After a rusted area has been sandblasted or chemically treated to kill the rust, the next step depends on what part of the car you're working on. If you're working on any part of the exterior body, patching and/or filling is usually required before going any further. Refer to the sequence of photos in this chapter for a step-by-step illustration of how to replace a rusted section of metal.

Once you've patched a panel, or if you've treated a rust spot on a part of the car other than the body, such as the chassis or an inner panel, then you'll want to look into some rust-prevention chemicals. These include special paints, such as Por-15 or Eastwood's Rust Encapsulator, both of which you can apply directly onto bare metal and even over rusted metal.

Undercoatings are an important consideration

Protective coatings and special fillers also fall into the rust treatment chemicals category. At my shop we use a variety of products from Evercoat-Fiberglass, SEM, POR-15 and Eastwood for both rust and regular repairs. The POR-15 paint and Eastwood Rust Encapsulator are specially formulated coatings that can be applied directly over rusted metal. I don't recommend that you leave rust spots on your car, but for some applications, such as chassis restoration and painting of the undercarriage and suspension components, these paints can be real time savers.

whenever a repair is made. No matter how thorough you are in removing rust and properly treating the metal, leaving the backside of the repair unprotected is an open invitation for rust to start again. As a general rule, whenever any type of repair work is performed to a car's body, always coat the backside of the repair with a rubberized undercoating or a rust-preventing paint.

Once you've revealed the extent of rust on your car's body panel, it's time to get your tools out and begin the surgical procedure. Much like a doctor removes a cancerous tumor from a vital organ, you must accurately assess the amount of cutting and patching that must be performed to totally eliminate the corrosion. If by chance you happen to leave even the tiniest spot of rust behind, like cancer, it will continue to grow until it once again becomes a hideous eyesore.

If you are lucky enough to catch body rot before it has a chance to eat through any part of the body, then you'll be performing the most basic of all rust repairs. Using a stiff wire wheel or a coated abrasive disc on a small right-angle grinder, you can prep the rusted area by removing the paint and topcoats on and around the spot of rust. Next comes the chemical treatment to dissolve and kill the remaining rust. After neutralizing the acid residue on the metal with baking soda and rinsing with water, you should be left with some black spots where the rust once was. Properly treated with the correct chemical, red oxide turns into black oxide — an inert and harmless compound that can be prepped and covered with a thin coat of body filler.

If you are replacing the rusted-out section of metal, the standard procedure is to cut out an area slightly larger than the rusted spot. Care must be taken to avoid cutting through any bracing or other parts that might be located behind the rust spot. The best way to avoid making any unwanted cuts is to visually inspect the cut path from both sides of the panel. If you cannot access the backside, you can still cut a section of metal out safely if you use the right tool and take your time.

Chapter Eight

Repair Without Paint

The system of PDR, or paintless dent repair, is simple by concept, but very difficult in practice. You will need a small amount of equipment, but a ton of experience to do it right.

Roof dents from hail can easily be removed with experience or some training.

Special picks all have smooth rounded tips for working the dents out in a rubbing or rotational pressing motion.

One dilemma that many owners of classic cars face at one time or another is how to make a repair to the body without affecting the originality and worth of the vehicle. A small dent or a mild crease on a custom-painted body is another situation that will make you wish there was some way of fixing the sheet metal without having to repaint it.

There are a few "N" words that you should learn, one is "N"ever use the word Bondo, "N"ever say "good enough" in front of a customer. And never, ever say "it will buff out." Classics and vintage cars are not to be taken lightly, and if you cannot do the job perfectly, or the customer will not cover the cost of a premium job, then you both would be better served if you just pass on the job.

I often fight this dilemma myself because of my eagerness to do certain jobs, such as movie work. For example, I always wanted to build a mechanical great white shark, and I got the opportunity a couple of years ago. I was so excited about project that I agreed to make the shark do a big list

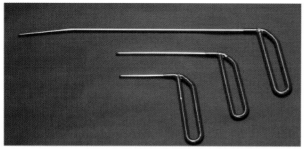

This is another tool that can also work on some dents, such as the small oilcan type.

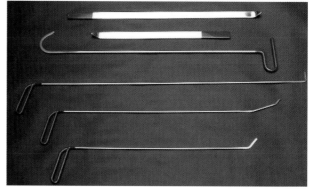

Six primary tools are included in this small paintless dent repair kit.

of extra things without adding to the cost of the shark. In other words, the shark got the best of me! But once I said yes, I was committed to it and had to see it through, even as the labor alone far exceeded the price I agreed to on the project. What I should have done was distance myself from the project and looked at it as just another job.

If you are doing the work for a profit, as are most people you should start seeing how long it takes to do certain projects so you can get a feel for charging customers for you skill.

Paintless Repairs

There is a "not so new system" out on the market called paintless dent repair and it is a way of using leverage and skill to remove dents from cars without having to use filler. The reason I bring it up is that it teaches you to read the dent and how to reverse the impact and iron the dent out by using your brain, not your muscles. There are a number of systems on the market that are all pretty similar. The process is mainly used for door dings caused by runaway shopping carts, kids on skateboards, or other minor mishaps. The system works best on small cosmetic blemishes that can be repaired in a matter of minutes in most cases. The technicians, as they are often called, will gain access to the area behind the dent and massage the metal back into place using slow wiping motions and light prying force on the back of the panel, "ironing the dent out" without damaging the outside painted surface. These technicians will study for many months to perfect this skill and wind up making a very decent living removing dents on cars with custom paint jobs. For car owners, a $50 dent repair sure beats a $2,000 to $4,000 bill for touching up a three-stage custom multicolored pearl paint job.

Small dime-size dents to full door panel dents can sometimes be removed in a matter of minutes. It's pretty amazing to watch a trained professional perform this trick. In many cases, there is no evidence a dent ever existed. And the only evidence in other cases it a small black plug in a door jamb indicating paintless dent removal was necessary. Paintless dent removal may be the least invasive way to

repair a dent. And for vehicles with custom paint jobs, paintless dent removal is often the only way to salvage the design. However, it is not an end-all cure and I would not expect you to run out and plop down $2,000 to $3,000 for the complete set of tool for the process until you learn a little more about it and its shortcomings. Yes, there are shortcomings and much of the training is in knowing what you can and cannot repair with the system.

The paintless tools and methods are not foolproof and they do have limitations as to the type and extent of damage that can be repaired with them. The only bad knowledge is the lack of knowledge (grasshopper), so a trip to a pointless dent repair shop is an education in and of itself and something I would encourage for everybody interested in paint and bodywork.

Depending on the dent and the skill of the operator, you may be able to remove dents up to 6 inches in diameter, but the biggest concern is how much of the vehicle's metal was stretched on impact. Stretched metal cannot be unstretched with any kind of pry bars and requires a different type of repair to get back into shape.

Another factor is the brittleness of the paint. Paint that is brittle may crack during the pointless dent repair. Some vehicles' coatings take years to reach a brittle stage, while other paints come out brittle from the factory. If brittle paint is a problem, using a heat gun to warm a dented area may help.

Gaining access to the area behind a dent is normally not a problem, but it can be on some cars. Although every dent can be accessed eventually, some may not be worth the effort. What is the point spending 20 hours getting access to back of a panel to remove a dent that only takes about 1 hour to fix from the font side with a bit of filler? That is, unless the car is a classic or custom and it absolutely has to be repaired correctly. Fixing a small dent in a hard-to-reach area is often tougher than fixing a large one.

While dents, dings and creases vanish in a matter of minutes at the hands of a pro with the proper tools, developing these skills is not an overnight feat. It takes a few months to learn the basics, and a few years months of continued training to become skilled at it. The absolute

This tool is sold by Eastwood and works by hot melting the center pin to the body. You simply turn the center screw to pull the dent out. This approach will not work with stretched metal, but it will pull a small dent out in some cases.

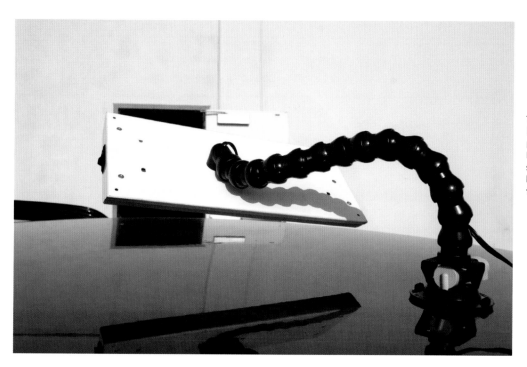

This light is an important tool for paintless dent repair. It sticks to the car via suction cup and can be maneuvered on a flexible arm.

best way to learn is to watch someone doing it or get a how-to video, then put in a ton of practice.

The tools needed for this type of repair are very specialized. A set of basic tools can cost $2,000, and investments of about $3,000 are required for more complete toolboxes. Most of the tools on the market are similar. Among the more important ones are:

➤ Rods with multiple ends bent into various angles, or a single rod with multiple tips and adjustable angles. These can provide access to damaged panels.

➤ A fluorescent light or a reflective board. These show every wave, dent and mark on a vehicle's body. Use the light to observe the dents and to mark your progress. As the dings disappear, the light's reflection on the vehicle improves. With the light, the tool's path is also monitored.

Another idea is to make a filter that goes in front of the light that has slits cut in it for casting parallel lines that will reflect on the surface of the car.

Access the Dents

Before agreeing to perform a paintless dent repair, most experts will verify that the technique will repair the vehicle. If the metal is stretched or gouged, or there is just too much damage, the "expert" will pass on it and suggest you visit a repair shop. However, even if they cannot remove the dent entirely they can improve it and this will translate into a lower repair cost at the body shop. If you are determined to get the damage repaired, try the paintless repair first and then continue form there. This will just make the rest of

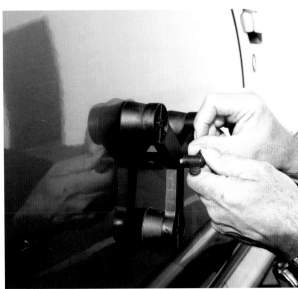

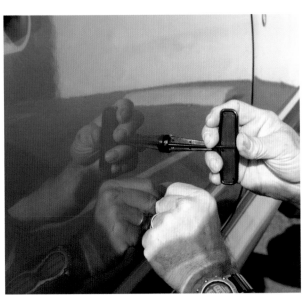

The Eastwood kit I'm using here does offer small dent repair and an affordable price and it will work for some small dents.

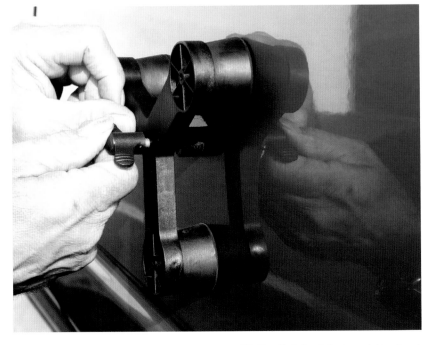

The dent kit has three different tools that will fit almost any area on a car's body.

the job easier and you can mix techniques as you go.

Once you have decided to repair a dent, you have to figure out how you are going to access the dent. Hoods and trunks are much easier to get at than doors, but doors can be approached from below and most have weep holes to allow moisture to escape. These holes are great access points for the rods to be inserted through. Front fenders are a snap to access on most cars, and rear quarter panels are also accessible through the trunk or rear passenger area. Repairing the hood or trunk frequently requires removing noise dampening pads found on the underside and working through and around the cross braces that are on the underside.

Working on a roof requires dropping part of the headliner to access the panel.

In a worst-case scenario you can drill holes to access the panel and plug the holes later with plastic plugs made for just such a situation.

Under the Hood

For dent removal under the hood you will be dealing with three things: the noise-dampening pad (if there is one), a brace that will almost certainly block the path to the damage, and the bonding caulk between the hood and the brace that will often not allow you to get your tool in place to perform the repair. The pad is usually not much of a problem. It is normally easy to remove. If it is glued in place you may need to cut it to gain access to the damaged metal of the hood.

One you have access to the back side of the dent you will need to secure the hood. One technique is to use an adjustable hood prop that will allow you to adjust the work height. Place the prop under the center of the hood and evenly space two motorcycle tie-down straps on each side of the prop. Adjust the straps so no movement is possible. Then you can slide the dent removal tool through the brace, using what was a former obstacle as a helpful point of leverage.

Door Dings

Doors are easy because there are so many access holes in a door that you can use, including the window slot that you will not have to drill any holes to pry against. If you use the window slot, be sure to place something against the window glass to spread the load and protect the glass from shattering.

Picking a Tool

Once access is established, select the proper tool. This will come with time and experience. I always hate it when someone says something like "use the right tool," especially when you are just learning and have no idea what the right tool is.

First, figure out which tool has the length you need to get from an access hole to the damaged area. Take into account the length, diameter and tip size when choosing the tool. The diameter should be as large as you can fit in the hole so the tool does not flex too much when prying with it. Don't use a tool that's too big, however, or you won't have room to move it around.

Let There be Light!

To start a repair, you will need a light source that will allow you to have a reflective surface to help locate the dent. For example, if the surface of the car is black and you hold a fluorescent light next to it you will see reflected straight lines on smooth, straight surfaces and clean, curved lines on shaped areas such as a fender. If there is a disruption in the fender, such as a dent or ding, the light reflection will give it away. It is best to have a light that you can mount on the car by a magnet or some other method so it can be positioned to allow you to view the reflection of the panel that you are about to repair. Position the light perpendicular to the damage. Working at an angle creates an optical illusion and makes it more difficult to locate the tip of the tool. Standing perpendicular to the dent is the beat method.

Now you can start the repair. The idea is to use repeating movements to duplicate the pressure that caused the damage in the first place. Remember, a lot of small pressures can equal a single large pressure. By applying pressure over and over again, you can slowly move the metal and paint back into its original position, in most cases without damaging the paint. It will take many soft pushes to reverse the damage because only a small amount of metal can be moved at a time, and this is where you will start to build a skill. You will no doubt get a feeling of satisfaction as you see the dent roll slowly out of the damaged area.

There are different types of damage and there is a preferred method for fixing each type. Oil can dents are reversed by slowly massaging the center of the damage. To repair a crease, apply pressure to the center of the crease using a motion that runs the length of the crease and slowly slide the tool along the crease until the dent is removed.

If you have a dent within a dent you should start with the smaller dent, repairing it to about 90 percent, then move out to the large dent. After the larger dent is repaired, move back to the smaller one and finish the 10 percent that was left over. The repair of the smaller dent may have been holding the larger dent in the panel,

The larger end of a teardrop-shaped dent should be repaired using the method for standard dents. Then the remainder of the dent can be treated as a crease and slowly worked out from the outside inwards.

Once the tip of the tool is located, move it to the center of the damage. Apply pressure in short, steady pulses. Watch the light bulbs reflection on the vehicle. You should see the wavy reflected line start to follow the curve of the repaired body as you push the metal back into shape. The light reflection will be your guide.

Remember, you will be removing the dent from the outside inward. To help you with this concept, visualize the dent as a large bicycle wheel. Divide the wheel in half as you place the tool at the "tire" area of this imaginary wheel. Now draw the tool form the tire area to the center "axle" portion of the pretend wheel. As you draw toward the center of the wheel you will be increasing the pressure on the tool.

As the dent start coming down in size, more force will be required to press it out. This is the point that you will have to be very careful to avoid pressing in the wrong area and adding to the damage. Keep the high pressure to the center of the dent and not the outer area, or you will distort the panel and have to resort to traditional methods of repair, including a repaint of the panel.

Also be very careful that the tool does not slip across the back of the panel, causing a crease that will be all but impossible to repair. Make sure the pivot point is not slippery. You may even place a rag over the edge of the metal to help guarantee that the tool does not slip. Move the tool in short controlled strokes.

After repairing a dent, you may be left with a few high spots. These can be easily pushed back flat again by using a small hammer and a tool that resembles a plastic punch or an oversized pencil. Some of these tools are designed with a variety of tip sizes. Another way to prevent high points is to wrap the rod tip with several layers of duct tape. This will help soften the tool's force on the area. Remove the tape when you are nearing completion of the repair to help you finish up.

Once the repairs are made using the paintless dent repair (PDR) method there is little chance to rectify errors. It is a skill that will need to be perfected before you ever start on a customer's car. However, for do-it-yourselfers who just want to work on their own cars as much as possible, it can be very beneficial to simply understand the basics and logic behind PDR. It is another tool in your arsenal of bodywork arsenal.

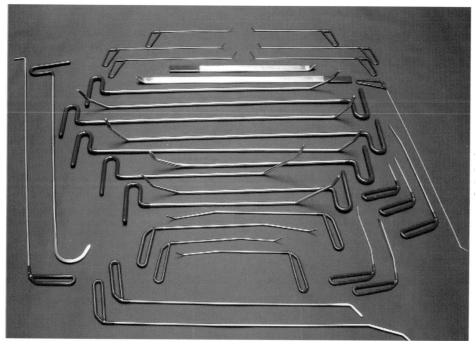

This a kit that includes almost every tool you will ever need to reach any part of the inner panels of a car or truck.

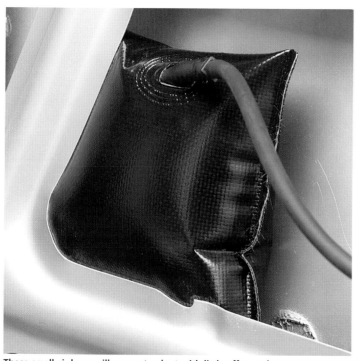
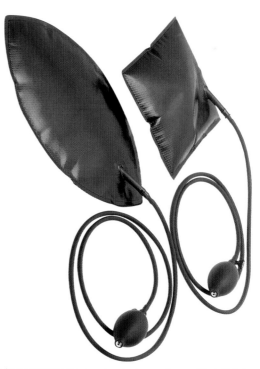

These small air bags will pop out a dent with little effort as long as you can get the bag between the panel and a brace of some kind. This is also sold through Eastwood.

Finishing Touches

If an access hole was drilled to allow the tool to be inserted you will need to seal it with either a sealant or a plastic plug. These are available at most body supply shops and automotive paint shops.

After a PDR you may need to wet sand the paint down and buff the area out, or, in a worst-case scenario, do a spot paint of the area.

A variety of paintless dent repair kits made by companies such as Dent Out and Dentool are available from Eastwood. These kits range in size from a simple starter kit to an elaborate professional systems complete with special lights, picks, hooks, bars, punches and rods. Keep in mind that some conventional body tools can serve double-duty as a paintless repair tool.

Chapter Nine

Paint Basics

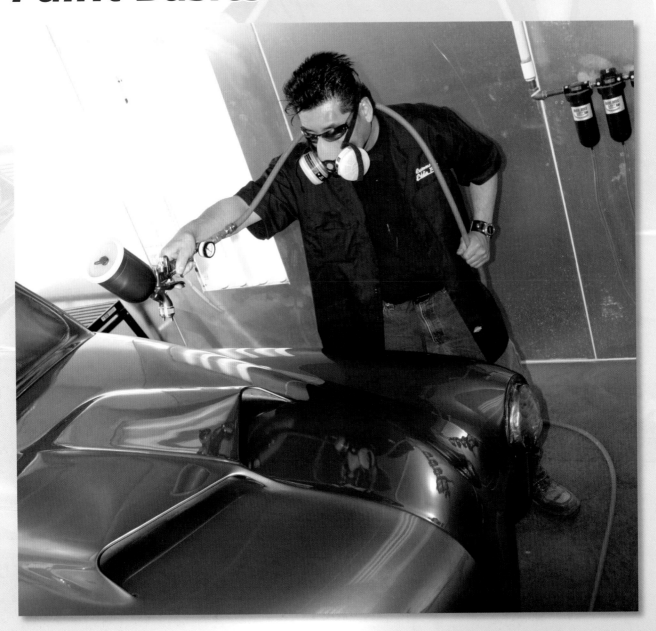

Eddie Paul's Paint & Bodywork Handbook

These three bikes all have different types and styles of paint, requiring different methods of application. You need to be ready for just about anything that comes down the road if you are going to be a painter.

A Brief and Not-So-Colorful History

The first recorded paint jobs were done by the cavemen as they found creative ways to decorate their caves while at the same time recording a little history. These crude but lasting paint jobs were applied in many ways, from fingers to makeshift brushes containing carefully plucked animal hairs. I wonder if these could be considered the first pinstriping brushes? In any event, the paintings were crude at best and colorful at the least.

In ancient Egypt, tombs were ornately decorated in paint, gold and silver. The paints and pigments used by the Egyptians demonstrated a huge technology leap. In fact, many of the colors and applications are difficult to duplicate with even today's technology. The lifespan of many of the coatings has far exceeded many of today's paints. The colors and combinations of colors indicate an amazing knowledge and control of pigments and powders and vehicle (liquid that allows the pigment to be brushed or sprayed). Today,

paint is used for both protection and decorating and the Egyptians use both to the fullest extent.

Centuries later as the automobile evolved, man early automakers offered color charts to potential buyers with only one color chip in it: black! As Henry Ford said, the customer could have "any color he wanted, as long as it was black." His quip summed up the attitude of the time — color was not an option. Like many of Ford's decisions, this was based on finance. Ford found that the pigment used in black for some reason allowed black enamel to dry faster than other colors, so, as far as he was concerned, black was the color of choice. At least it wasn't that mustard yellow that turned out to be the fast-drying color?

Every car Ford painted needed to sit in drying warehouses for days. Wayward rodents running in the rafters would occasionally dislodge a handful of dust into the wet paint, forcing the car to be re-sanded and painted again. Even with the meticulous mixture and application of the paint, the average paint job was only good for about three years. Paint and the painting process still had a lot of evolving to do.

For Pixar's *CARS*, we had to paint Sally the Porsche to Porsche standards (which are very high).

On the other end of the spectrum we painted the tow truck "Mater" with a flat, multicolored, rust-based tan (bugs included).

Lightning McQueen received a simple red paint job, but what set it off was all the vinyl wrap, trim and details we added to the car. Lightning was made out of ABS plastic that we vacuum formed just for Pixar/Disney.

Paint Basics

We paint with the best HLVP spraying equipment from Devilbiss, Sharpe and Sata.

Mixing paint or primer requires a filter holder. The filter holder was taken out here while we added the catalyst to the primer.

A paint mixing bench can become a bit disorganized if it's not maintained each day. There are lots of items and chemicals involved in the painting process.

Paint is made from three main components: a binder, diluents and additives. Out of the three, only the binder is absolutely required. Without the binder the paint would never dry. The diluent is the viscosity control (how thick the paint is when it is applied) and it will "flash off" and disappear as the paint dries. Most of these diluents are commonly referred to as solvents, such as alcohols, ketones, esters, glycol and even water. Anything else is just the additives, which included the pigment (color). Most pigments are powders and will not dissolve in the binders but are suspended in them, requiring mixing before the application of the paint onto the car. Most pigments are heavier than the binders, so they will sink to the bottom of the can pretty fast. Constant agitation is sometime required, especially on heavy metalflakes. Other additives can include dyes, thickeners, catalysts, texturizers, flatteners — almost anything that will make the paint behave a certain way.

Early enamel paints were composed of the seeds of flax plant and the pine tree. They were crushed to produce linseed oil, which was mainly used as a metal protector in

I had my booth in the shop years ago, but found it used up too much interior space. Now I have it outside, covered by a shed.

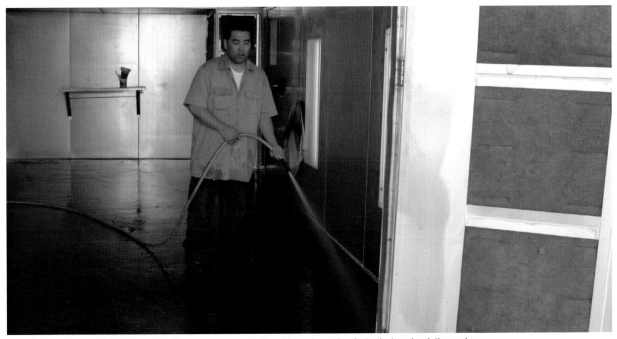

I put the booth on a slight hill to help the water run off to the side and out the drain during the daily washes.

many parts of the world as a paint. Baked enamel appeared around 1915 and, as the name indicates, it requires baking in a large oven to set up fast. It will dry if not baked, but it takes much longer. The development of synthetic enamel required high temperatures but lessened drying time to about an hour. Black was about the only color offered until about 1923, and it was known as black baked enamel. Lacquer (nitrocellulose paint) came to the auto industry in 1923 as a Satin Finish Duco. In 1924, Pontiac was the first to finish cars in Duco. "True Blue" was the only color

available at the time. By the end of the year, the entire GM line was covered in Duco, as were many other automaker's cars. In 1928, Ford jumped on the Duco wagon, which drove Ford nuts due to the fact that GM owned 39 percent of DuPont stock. This was corrected by the Justice Department as GM was forced to divest the DuPont stock, which surely made Henry happy.

Ford then switched back to "Alkyd Synthetic Enamel." Metallic paint was introduced in the late 1930s to early 1940s and was available on a limited basis on the 1940

A small counter is handy to have in the spray booth. You can use it to mix paint without having to leave the booth.

Putting a car on stands helps the painter get under the wheel wells.

Brian has found a small run and a spot of dust that will be magnified if it's painted over. In this instance, he block sanded it down flat and smooth and later re-sprayed the white base.

While spraying a base coat you'll often find small spots that will need repair. We sometimes have to block sand the area down again, allowing us one last chance to get the finish perfect.

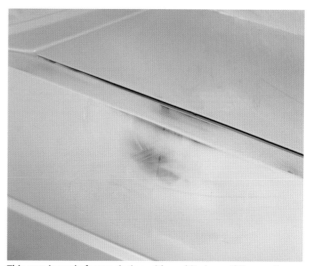

This area is ready for repainting with a white base. If the sanding process had gone down to the bare metal, the area would have to be re-primed before being re-sprayed with the white base.

Packard. Metallic paint used metal powder in combination with traditional paint. It highlighted the shape of the curves better than any other non-metallic paints, but the powder was aluminum and the paint had to be clear coated or it would dull quickly from oxidation. If the clear was sanded or buffed too much, the paint job would have to be re-cleared.

In the 1950s candy, or translucent, finishes debuted. They were a concoction of more clear than color over a base of either black, silver, gold or white. And this, too, required a top coat of clear. Some of the early attempts to make candy paint involved inks that were found to blotch when exposed to sunlight. Credit for the first original candy paint job is co-claimed by Joe Bailon, Emmit Glasglow and George Barris, but it appears that candy was being worked on independently by a few different people at the same time in different shops.

Pearl paint followed in about 1956, shortly after candy

The base is now complete and ready for the Candy Orange color coat and later the clear.

Rubber sanding blocks for color sanding are pretty much necessity items. You will get a few runs in the beginning and have to sand them out. During wet sanding, they are the best tool to form the sandpaper around.

paint and the first pearls were made and sold exclusively from Japan from powered fish scales. These paints had a half life of about 20 minutes, so they quickly blotched and turned yellow in the hot sun. Later, ground-up abalone shells were tested with the same diminutive existence. Finally, the pearls of today were constructed from crushed mica, giving them a life as long as the binder they are suspended within.

Since mica is a mineral and not organic it is not susceptible to fading in sunlight, as were the fish parts.

Metalflake was introduced in 1960 by the Dobeckmun Co., a division of Dow Chemical, and later became Metalflake Inc. I might note that the name "Metalflake" itself is a bit deceiving as the metal flakes are not metal at all, but very small rectangles of mylar that are dyed to the desired color and sold in a small bag to be mixed in with the clear just before spraying. A special gun was also invented that constantly agitates the mylar using air pressure from the air line to turn a small mixing arm inside the spraygun cup. If the Metalflake is not kept agitated, it will settle to the bottom of the cup in minutes and ruin the mixture of flake to clear. I wonder, why they don't make the mylar with the same specific gravity as the clear so it stays suspended without constant agitation?

Epoxies and polyurethanes were next on the evolutionary road. These are simply catalyzed paints not unlike fiberglass resin. They dry much harder and faster than paint of the past.

All in all, not a whole lot has happened in the automotive paint industry in recent years. A few new colors and a few new and better paints, but to be honest, the paint and finishing market has lagged way behind the rest of the world and could use a push. Who knows, maybe this book will inspire somebody to come up with a better paint. Maybe in the future paint will be mixed in with the metal of the car or have a way of changing by flicking a switch to a totally different color. The future is limited only by our imagination.

Eddie Paul's Paint & Bodywork Handbook

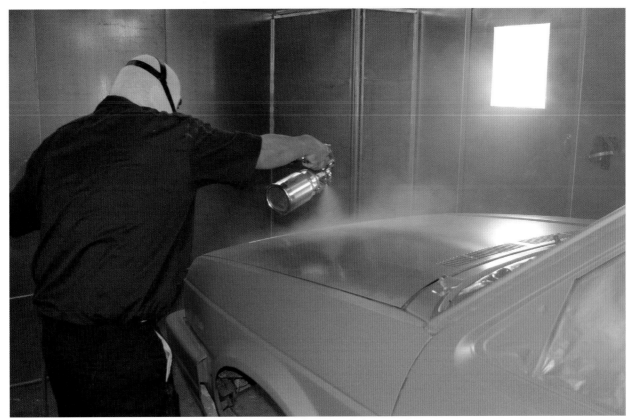

Candy is not an easy color to paint. It is transparent, and any imperfection in the base coat is easy to see.

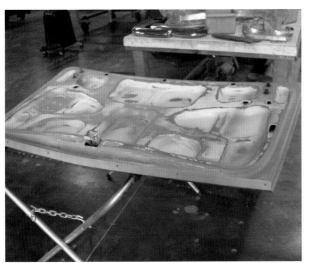

These are what we call "jambs." These parts or areas have to be painted first and should get as much attention as the outside of the car. It's helpful if these parts can be removed for painting.

Preparing for Paint

Getting ready to paint involves as much psychology as it does physical preparation and proper equipment. All the work you have done to repair and prepare the car's body will culminate within a few hours in the spray booth. If you did everything right, you can still destroy a paint job with one wrong swipe of the gun. Or a single kamikaze bug on a death mission can cut a path across the hood bigger than you would ever believe. Or that one piece of molding that you did not blow out properly will spread

huge quantities of sand across your newly painted roof. Or maybe you just did not get the mixing ratio between the paint and the reducer exactly correct and the paint either came out too thin with runs all over the side of the car, or you did not add enough solvent and the paint comes out as dry as powder.

When you are banging a car into a reasonable shape and transforming it from a beat-up wreck into something decent, you'll never have a crowd standing around to inspect your workmanship. But the second the door of the booth

A good strainer for the paint and a good spray mask will keep the paint, and your lungs, clean.

opens, everyone in the shop, and maybe a few relatives you have not seen in years, will be standing there to critique every square inch of the newly painted surface, looking not for the great job you did, but for the one tiny mistake you may have made. The chances of obtaining a perfect paint job are not good, so get it out of you mind and just try to get a good paint job. That little bit of stress reduction can help tremendously, your heart rate will be lower and the job will come out much better than if you were aiming for perfection. This will not keep birds out of your booth, but you will be more relaxed.

You can never have enough filter to clean the air before it gets to your gun. We have enough with this DeVilbiss Clean Ar system.

Eddie Paul's Paint & Bodywork Handbook

Brian uses a plastic bucket to premix the paint a gallon at a time and then transfers it through a strainer to the awaiting spraygun cup.

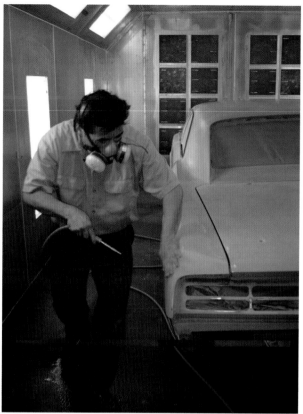

Blow the car or bike off at every occasion, just to get rid of that last piece of dust that is hiding under something. If you are using a booth, be sure to keep the fans on during the blowing-off process.

Painter's Check List

- ➤ Think the job through from start to finish, and get your equipment and materials in order
- ➤ Be neat and organized
- ➤ Check the filters
- ➤ Clean the booth or area
- ➤ Clean the area around the booth
- ➤ Check the hoses
- ➤ Test the gun
- ➤ Know the mixing ratio
- ➤ Check the temperature
- ➤ Make sure you have the right solvents
- ➤ Have tweezers handy for dust particles

Sanding

When I started out in bodywork I was basically self taught, finding any information I could in magazines, books and talking to other painters and body men. I would even hang out at body shops and just watch guys work to see what tools and materials I would need for the job. I slowly got into it by "word of mouth advertising" until I was hammered with jobs and the phone was distracting me from work. I remember making a vow that I would never change a bid and jack the price up on the customer as many had done with me in the past. The rule was: If I bid it, I would stick to the bid no matter what, even if the job was underbid. After all, that was my fault for underbidding it.

And most of my bids were "right on," but one day I received a call from a guy named Abe and the conversation went something like this: "I hear you can paint my tank," to which I asked "what color?" He responded, "Army drab with a star on each side... how much?" I said "about $200." He then said "I also hear that you will honor your bid?" then I started to get suspicious. "Is the tank damaged, because bodywork is extra." He stated, "not a dent." I then asked if it had rust, to which he again responded "not a bit." So the deal was struck and I told him to bring it over, which he said would take about an hour.

One hour later my house shook (I was working out of my garage at the time) and I went to the front window to see what was making the noise.

I had been suckered by Abe! As I looked out the window I saw the tank that I had bid on. It was a tank, but not a gas tank. It was an Army tank! It show up with faded paint, a cannon, a machine gun and a faded star on each side of the turret.

Just the cost of the paint alone would put me in debt for quite some time, but a bid is a bid, and I did say I would not change my price. What the heck, it would look good

Paint Basics

Even though we seem to have every air tool known to man in our shop, we still use the long boards for finishing the surface of a custom car. There is no tool that replaces the human feel for shaping a compound curve on a car.

With the major bodywork complete, we were ready to start this paint job. The job required a lot of last-minute block sanding. We used 600-grit wet or dry paper for the final sanding before the car went to the booth.

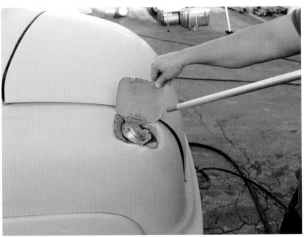

The Merc was then taken outside and blown off before paint. After all, it had about two years of dust accumulated in the cracks and crevices of the frame and inner body.

in my scrapbook, and later on Joe Walsh's *There Goes The Neighborhood* album cover.

What does this have to do with sanding? Well, that is how I saved my butt on the job. Painting is fairly easy. It takes skill, but not a lot of time. Sanding takes time, but not a lot of skill. So I told Abe that the price did not include sanding, just painting! "Checkmate," I thought. If he wanted sanding, it would be extra. But Abe was sharp, I will give him that. His response was "then don't sand it, grind it! After all, it is a tank." This guy was good.

Tree days and 36 grinding disks later I was ready to apply the 16 gallons of OD (Olive Drab) paint to the freshly ground 1/4-inch-thick hardened steel plate. If I had to sand the tank down to steel I would have had a month's worth of labor into it, but because it was not thin sheet metal I got away with grinding the old paint off without warping the steel. This helped, but I still lost my butt on the job. But then a bid is a bid.

No one likes sanding, but it is what separates the men from the boys in bodywork. It is lonely and boring and you will remove every hint of your fingerprints even on a quick job, but the end result of a paint job relies mostly on the quality of the sanding. Any shortcuts will be eternally cast in the finish for the life of the paint job. Of course, those flaws will be pointed out by some snot-nose kid that walks by and says, "hey, look Dad, he has a scratch under his paint. Poor prep, should have sanded better. I would have used 1600 grit!"

One tool that may help is a Walkman or iPod for the long hours of solitary sanding in the shade. This will at least give you contact with other humans as you sand your fingers to the bone. In the end, though, the sanding process, if done correctly, will make the difference between a show car and an average paint job that anyone can produce.

Most people are anxious to get the paint on a car and do not want to stand and sand, but if you are not prepared to spend the time sanding, it's best not to even start a job. Try to look at sanding as the creative part of the job and the paint as the easy part. After all, a run can be repaired by color sanding or rubbing, or even a spot touch-up, but bodywork can't be fixed later — it has to be right before the paint is applied. Remember, when your paint is finished, most people are looking not at what a great job you did, but for a flaw in the job. Recently, I was at a car show and no fewer than 20 people came by my booth and told me about a Rolls Royce in the same show with a chip in the paint job. They all seemed to take pride in the fact that they found a flaw in what was otherwise thought of as a "perfect car."

Sanding is all about feel and finding the imperfections before someone else does, so try to make a game out of it, not a chore. Try to catch and correct all the mistakes and small dings or scratches until you can check the whole body over and not find one. Then challenge a friend to check your work to see if they can find a flaw. There will still be imperfections no matter how careful you are, and they can point them out to you.

The Nitty-gritty of Sandpaper

What is the meaning of grit when it pertains to sandpaper, Grasshopper? An old wiseman once asked, so Grasshopper looked it up on the Internet and, being the smart grasshopper he was, he not only found the answer within minutes, but found the answer to be wrong! (True, the Internet is only as accurate as the input of the dumbest donor). the Sandpaper 101 Web site (yes, there is a Web site on sandpaper) stated that the grit is measure by "how many grains of sand will fit into a 1 inch square" What it should have said is the number of grains of sand that fit on a 1-inch line, not in a 1 inch square. Let me explain: If you lay down large grains of sand on a line that is one inch long there would be, more or less, 16 grains of sand for 16 grit paper if you filled a 1-inch square with these large grains of sand you would have about 256 grains of sand. Further, if you laid down 3,000 grains of sand on a line for 3,000-grit sandpaper and then filled a square with the small grains of sand you would have 9,000,000 grains of sand in 1-square inch of sandpaper. Have you ever heard of 9-million grit paper?

Sandpaper grit is a linear measurement, not an area measurement. If you doubt me, go out and measure your sandpaper grains, but start with the 3,000-grit paper — anyone can measure the 16-grit paper. Report back to me next year.

Rating Sandpaper

Sandpaper is rated as follows:

36-grit is considered coarse-grit paper and is used for removing dead birds and stripping paint form the surface of a car. It can be used during bodywork to rough out the body filler after using a grinder or cheese grader.

80-120-grit is called medium-grit paper and is the next stage in removing the scratches that were put in by the 40-60 grit paper. This paper will start giving you the shape for the finish panel.

180-grit is used before the first coat of primer. Primer will fill in the scratches from 180.

280-320 grit is considered extra fine and is normally a "wet or dry" paper, but should only be used wet. This is used to take the initial primer down for the second coat of primer.

360-600 grit is be used just before the base coat is applied. This will be your last chance to catch any imperfections in the paint.

A good-quality respirator will fit well around your face. If you smell paint while painting, stop and check your mask. If the mask is sealed and the filters are correct, you should not smell any fumes from the paint. An OSHA-approved respirator fit test kit can be used if you're not sure about the fit.

Chemical Safety

As is the case with most chemicals, always take the right safety precautions when working with all paint-related materials. When I was young, safety was not a big issue. In fact, I don't remember my auto shop teacher ever telling me to wear a respirator mask, safety glasses or hearing protection, which may account for my poor vision and bad hearing today. To stress the importance of using precautions when working with chemicals, I have another lovely story that may drive the point home even better.

I was 16 at the time and working on one of my cars — I think it was a 1950 Dodge that was running bad. I decided to rebuild the carburetor and purchased some carburetor dip, sold in a one-gallon can. Midway through the cleaning project my hands started to burn, so I washed them off in cold water, to no avail. As time passed, the pain increased to the point that I tried to call my dad at work to ask him what to do, but I couldn't get my swollen fingers into the holes in the rotary phone.

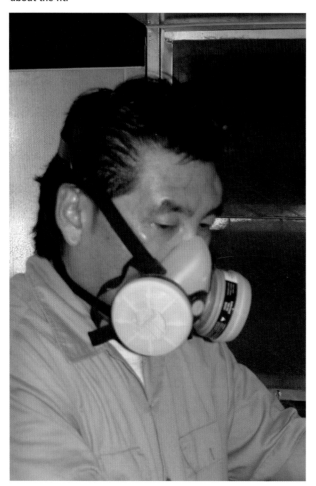

Soon, the swelling got so bad my hands were close to twice the size they had been when I started the job and the skin was starting to peel. I kept soaking them in water and eventually poured baking soda on them to neutralize the effects of the acid. Within a few days the swelling started to go down and I believe I can go on record as inventing the first chemical peel! Boy, did my hands look good for a while.

I did learn a few lessons that day. One was to read instructions on the can, the other was to wear gloves when working with chemicals. I am always hounding my crew

Eddie Paul's Paint & Bodywork Handbook

Masking is another area that you should never rush. Here we have already removed the windows and windshield and painted under them, then had them re-installed. It is better to tape short than long. For example, if the tape allows the rubber to show a little and you get paint on the rubber you can later clean it off. But if tape hangs over the rubber and onto the body, you will have to touch up the area with paint later.

A spray booth is an asset that you will need if you get serious about painting cars, and this is a good one to start with. It is from Tools USA and came by truck to our door. It is in a kit form that only took a few days to assemble. It came with filter and lights, although we had to buy the bulbs. This booth has a built-in table as well as the exhaust fan.

This booth has a built-in table as well as the exhaust fan. It also come with intake and exhausts filters.

to put on a mask, hearing protection or even gloves. I have first aid kits all around the shop and only wish someone would have taught me some bit of safety when I was young. Common sense dictates that if a chemical will remove grease or paint from a metal surface it should be handled with a lot of caution, in a well ventilated area and always with gloves.

Another time I was working over at Bruce Caldwell's house. At the time Bruce was a writer at *Hot Rod* magazine and was having me help him build a project car. I had showed up to help him pull the engine out of his '65

Mustang, which is a bit of a messy job, but one that had to be done before we could get on with the rest of the car's modifications.

I was walking up the driveway to his garage behind his house and was thrown into a fit of laughter by what I saw: Bruce had out of the back door of his house to help clean the engine off and he had donned his appropriate safety gear (in his mind): a set of large goggles under his full face shield, a set of full coveralls, large gloves and safety boots, ear plugs and helmet.

I was wearing a T-shirt and jeans. He was so "safetyed" out that he could barely move, and in fact was a danger to himself as well as me as he could not hear or see well and spent much of his time adjusting his safety gear. It did not take long for him to remove the gear a little at a time until he was dressed the same as I was — a T-shirt and jeans. At this point, we got a lot done, got real dirty and had fun. I'm sure that the bright summer sun also helped convince him to ditch some of his safety gear.

You don't have to overdo the safety thing — just resort to common sense when you are doing something that has an inkling of danger attached to it, or the faint smell of any kind of harmful chemistry.

The Paint Booth

I used to do a lot of custom cars for *Hot Rod* magazine as well as many of the other automotive magazines on the market; this was between the many movie projects I

The booth bench is a must because you need a place to set your gun and paint during the process. This is just the right spot — between the exhaust filters where the air flow is at a minimum.

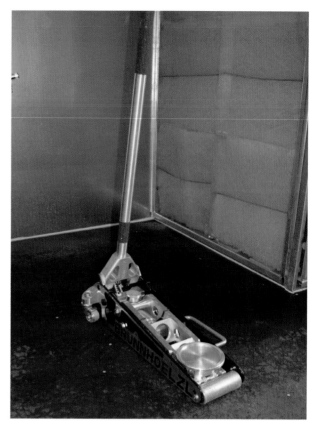

Sometimes we keep a jack in the booth for lifting the car, removing the wheels and tires, and getting the car on jack stands.

had going on, and these were referred to as "project cars" and were owned by the editors and writers of the different magazines. One of these project cars was owned by Bruce Caldwell, who was the feature editor of *Hot Rod* at the time and later became a freelancer working for many magazines and a few of the book companies. In any event, he moved from southern California to Woodinville, Washington and was still doing project cars, one of which was a '69 Camaro. It was a basic "book car" that was going to be the subject of one of his new how-to books. Bruce would buy an old junk car and do a step-by-step restoration from the ground up, from the engine rebuild to bodywork and paint. This is where I came in. Bruce called me and asked if I would be willing to come up to his place and paint the car for him. I said, "Sure got a booth and a gun?" His response: "No." So, I grabbed a spray gun, loaded up some sandpaper and a spare regulator. He agreed to get some plastic and 2 x 4 studs at the local lumberyard, and he had a hammer and nails. A co-worker and I flew up to Woodinville on a Friday evening, built a makeshift booth out of wood and clear plastic and proceeded to paint Bruce's car in the middle of the forest — appropriately, in Woodinville! The car came out great and made in into few magazines and on a cover. The point is that you don't have to have fancy equipment to paint a car. In fact, in many areas you are allowed to paint a car in your driveway. I wouldn't recommend it, but it is legal.

Spray booths are not that expensive and can sometimes be rented. Many body shops have them and will rent them

Equipment that you use for painting, such as jack stands, needs to be dust free or you will get dirt into your paint.

out on weekends for extra cash, so if you are interested in doing some painting, check around and see what is around you. If you are determined to have your own booth, there are options. We recently got a great booth via the internet from Tools USA. It was shipped to us and we assembled it within a few days. This is the way to go if you are working on cars for more than just a hobby. There are many booths on the market and you can have just about whatever you want in the way of filtering, lighting and setups for doors and air flow.

Once we got the car in the booth, this job went well. The process took about a gallon of paint and two gallons of clear. Brian did not go for the "high shine" finish in the booth, as he knew that would risk a potential run in the paint and the car was going to be buffed out completely anyway.

Here Brian demonstrates good painting technique with the gun perpedicular to the surface.

We jam and paint the edges first as we go around a car, allowing the paint in these areas to set up a bit before painting the larger flat areas. This gives us a chance to control the paint in the hard-to-reach areas first, then get into the simpler flatter areas last.

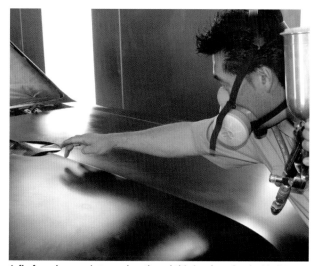

A fly found a way into my booth and this is where he decided to land. Keep a set of tweezers handy for just such an unwanted guest.

The base is black, the color is HOK Kkameleon and the clear will make it shine as well as protect it from the elements. This is a traditional three-stage paint job.

The Basics of Spraying

Learning to get the paint from a gun onto a surface without it sagging, running or being too dry is not a skill, it is an art and an art that can only be perfected by **practice, practice, practice**. Even after numerous practice sessions you still may not be able to acquire the touch. Your first paint job will not be a pretty sight, and your second or third jobs probably won't be award winners, either. If you stick with it, you'll probably get very good at buffing, because you'll have a lot of imperfections to try to fix. But stick with it. Remember that the early cars had their paint applied by brush and were sanded and rubbed out, so it can be done.

Spraying can be practiced on odd shapes such as bicycle frames and tool boxes — almost anything in your shop or garage that needs a new coat of paint. Paint anything that gives you spray time and an opportunity to work on your skills. Once the word is out that you are a painter, all your friends will want you to do a spot job of complete paint job for them. After you do a couple of nice paint jobs, there will be no shortage or work coming in for you to practice on. Oh yeah, and make them buy the paint.

Equipment is obviously a key component in paint work and you will want have a good-quality gun to shoot a good-quality paint job in a timely manner. That is not to say you can't get good results with an inexpensive gun, but it will take longer if you figure in the time it takes to fix a few runs and rub out a few dry spots. So the gun issue boils down to simple economics: What you save on a gun will cost you in quality and extra time. Heck, you could paint with a brush and then spend many, many hours sanding and rubbing the paint to a flawless finish and not have spent a dime on a gun. Or, you could buy a good quality gun, take the time to learn how to use it well, then spray a coat or paint that is good the first time and does not need hours of sanding, rubbing and touch-up.

Brian holds the air hose with his left hand to keep it from hitting the paint while he sprays.

HVLP Guns

There are all kinds of gadgets that will spray paint. There are pressure pots, gravity-feed guns, siphon guns, low and high pressure guns, big guns, small guns down and many different varieties of air brushes. What we will focus on here is the **HVLP Gravity Spray** gun. The HVLP just stands for "High Volume Low Pressure." The HVLP gun has gained popularity in the last 20 some years and was designed to keep the majority of the paint on the car and not in the air while utilizing the least amount or air to perform this task. In the beginning there was quite a learning curve as we all grumbled and complained about the guns and how we liked the old ones that really put out the paint. Well, the gun manufacturers listened and kept redesigning the guns to the point that they are today, and either they are better now, or we finally learned how to use them. Today, you can now lay down a pretty decent paint job with only 10 to 20 psi, something unheard of 20-some years ago.

Handling the Gun

The typical spray gun has a few knobs that can be turned in or out to increase or decrease this or that, giving the painter an unlimited number of options over air pressure, paint volume, flow, ratio of paint to air and amount of trigger pull. Some of the guns, like the SATA, are even digital (as far as the air pressure is concerned). Guns are made from aluminum, magnesium and even plastic, but most of the designs are basically the same. Control of the paint flow does not stop at the gun you will also have controls at the air compressor and water traps as well as pipes and elbows along the way. Just one 90-degree elbow will affect the final pressure a small amount, so if you have a bunch of them in the line along the way, it could make a huge difference in the gun's performance. Don't work with old hoses, either. I have seen a flap of rubber on the inside of a hose block the air supply and cause a few painters to scratch their heads.

If you look at the typical spray gun, you will notice the highest and most rearward portion of the gun has a small knob that can be turned in or out. This controls the spray pattern. The pattern can go from an elongated oval to a round pattern and back by simply turning the knob.

Below that is a fluid control knob that controls the amount of paint that exits the nozzle by determining the amount of trigger pull you have — the further you pull the trigger, the more fluid you get out the nozzle. It is really just a way of mechanically stopping you from pulling the trigger too far.

Now if you look down near the bottom of the handle where the air line hooks up, you should (better) have an air pressure regulator with a knob to control the amount of air pressure you have coming into the gun. Many states limit this amount of air pressure to 10 psi (over this pressure I

You can see the smooth even finish after the clear has been applied to the body. The real gloss will come from buffing the paint after color sanding it down to a perfect finish.

guess they assume air kills people, or something), so start with 10 psi. Once you have paint in the gun, pull the trigger slowly as you slowly turn the air regulator in. What you are looking for is how low you can get the incoming air pressure and still achieve full atomization of the paint. This will be the air pressure setting to use for that type of paint.

It may all seem simple, but between the three controls you have many different settings. Pay attention and make notes on the settings so you can keep things straight as you switch brands and types of paint. Remember, most of the paint companies print the desired setting on the can or in the paperwork that accompanies that product.

Patterns are the consequences of the settings: good settings = good patterns, bad settings = bad patterns, and patterns are what make a good paint job. A good pattern is elongated and even and consistent, laying down the proper thickness of paint throughout the entire pattern. Not more on one end or the other, but the same thickness through the full length of the pattern. A well-designed spray gun operates somewhat like a carburetor that is set to get the perfect atomization for the perfect burn. Unless you really know what you are doing, don't start re-drilling your gun's nozzle to get more paint out of the gun. The manufacturers have different nozzles available for different paints. Check with them if you need a special tip for a special job.

Spray patterns can be changed and I often do change them, depending on what I am painting. I may bring the

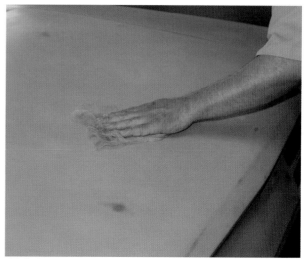

This little area was found on the roof just before we pushed the car into the booth. It had to be repaired, but 30 minutes later we were right back on track.

fan width down (turning the top knob inward) for a bike frame so I do not waste paint, but this means I am putting out much more paint in that smaller area so I will have to cut down so I will turn my control knob in a few turns to limit the paint volume.

I also rotate my tip (cap of the gun) when I paint a vertical surface such as the A, B or C pillars of the cars. I don't like to tilt my gun when I paint, I would rather rotate

Now the fun begins. The entire car has to be color sanded with fine wet or dry sanding paper.

Color sanding will take a whole day, if you are lucky, and will wear your fingerprints off. We add a bit of soap to the water to keep the sandpaper from sticking.

the tip or cap instead of the whole gun. When spraying a typical pattern down the side of the car you will need to start at the top and spray a single pattern down the side of the car with the middle of the spray pattern at the top edge of the car's top edge. This way, when you overlap the next successive pattern you will wind up with exactly two coats on the entire side of the car. If you would start with the top of the first spray pattern at the top of the car and proceed to overlap the next coat 50 percent of the first pattern and each pattern after that, your first spray pattern would only have a single coat a the top 50 percent and double coats the rest of the way down the side of the car.

The most important aspect of spraying technique is to be able to see the paint lay down as you spray. If you can't see how the particles atomize and lay down, it's like shooting in the dark. Learn to read the paint and get used to the look and feel of the paint as it hits the car's surface. Does it look dry or runny? Is it shiny, or dull and flat looking? Does it look constant from one panel to the next, or is it different from one to the next? Can you tell where you started the pattern and where you stopped, or is the paint seamless as it should be.

You will only learn by doing. No amount of reading will give you the feel, and you will only learn by making mistakes. When I was starting out I had no training and had to learn on the cheap using a gun with a small clunky compressor without a filter system. I learned in a hurry how to diagnose and repair paint mistakes. I could spot a

problem before it happened, but could do little to prevent it. Now, of course, we have the best equipment and a few years under our belts, but still have some problems as we switch brands from time to time. I still, on occasion, see the look of panic on Brian's face when a particular paint he is using doesn't react the same as a previous paint did with the same pressure and conditions. He always gets a handle on it and finishes the job, and when I ask him "how did it go with the new paint?" he always answers "great, no problem!" Yeah, sure. Even the experts have problems, they just have the experience to overcome them.

Proper HVLP gun technique is the last thing on most new painter's minds, but it's the most important thing to learn in the beginning, something that takes a lot of practice to master. Ideally, you want to keep the gun 6 inches from the surface of what you are spraying, and the gun must stay perpendicular to the entire surface as you move it along at a consistent rate of travel. Now, this may sound simple, but try it — it's tougher than it sounds. Combine this with the gun having to be shut off at the end of each stroke and started up (pulling the trigger) as the stroke reverses back down the panel, and you'll find there is some real coordination involved.

I have found that the best way to practice is to go very slowly with an empty gun and just air paint a car to get the feel of the gun and the motion. Every so often stop and measure how far off the surface you are. If you almost touch the surface with the nozzle of the gun you would

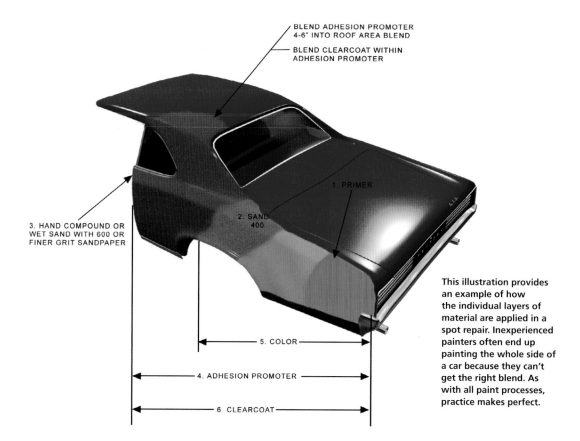

BLEND ADHESION PROMOTER
4-6" INTO ROOF AREA BLEND

BLEND CLEARCOAT WITHIN
ADHESION PROMOTER

1. PRIMER

2. SAND
400

3. HAND COMPOUND OR
WET SAND WITH 600 OR
FINER GRIT SANDPAPER

5. COLOR

4. ADHESION PROMOTER

6. CLEARCOAT

This illustration provides an example of how the individual layers of material are applied in a spot repair. Inexperienced painters often end up painting the whole side of a car because they can't get the right blend. As with all paint processes, practice makes perfect.

have created some major runs. It shouldn't take long to get the idea and soon you will be ready to load up a gun and try it with paint. I like to practice on odd-shaped objects such as tubing, and things that are round, such as barrels. Practicing on a flat surface is pretty easy. Practicing on a curved surface will accelerate the learning curve.

Spot Repairs

Many painters will tell you that performing a spot repair is more difficult than spraying a complete car. While a complete job may involve more labor, there are certain aspects of spot painting that can only be fully appreciated by an experienced refinisher.

Painting a complete car is certainly not without its share of potential pitfalls and problems but, for the most part, these are predictable and easier to avoid than those associated with spot painting. Unfortunately, the variables of spot painting are so numerous that we couldn't possibly cover every situation in detail. However, once you understand the basic procedures involved with spot painting, you'll be more able to handle whatever job might come your way.

An easy spot repair usually consists of repainting a solid non-metallic color on a late-model car. A solid color on a late-model car can usually be matched with accuracy, or can be purchased as a "factory pack" premix. Another easy spot repair is a panel that must be repainted. A valance, front fender or any section of a car that can be masked off

Many shops use 1,500-grit paper for color sanding.

separately from the remaining car body eliminates the need for blending. The blend of a spot repair and the match of the color are the two critical factors of a spot repair.

Certain colors are more difficult to match than others and as you gain more experience with different types of repairs, you'll find out what colors are hard to match and which ones are easy. I've found that metallics in general are always more difficult to match than solids because the variables are greater. Not only are there more toners in the

After one more inspection of the surface to see if we missed anything, this car looks ready to buff.

formula that the paint mixer must accurately measure, but the application of a metallic involves making sure that the paint particles lay down exactly like the existing paint does. This means that your spraying technique and air pressure at the gun are extremely critical. For example, a lower pressure tends to darken a metallic, while a higher pressure lightens the tone.

In the accompanying illustration, you can see the left rear quarter panel of a car. The rear quarter panel almost always involves blending, due to the fact that there is no clean break-off point where it can be masked off. Most quarter panels are part of the pillar and roof section of a car, unless it is a convertible model. So, if a very small area of a quarter-panel must be repainted, the goal should be to confine the repair to the smallest area possible without having to paint additional sections of the car unnecessarily.

Perhaps the easiest way to describe how to perform a spot repair with minimal confusion is that each coat of material is applied in overlapping layers. This begins with the repair itself. Because paint must be spotted in, it is important to keep the working area of the repair to a minimum. Allowing your bodywork to spread out will increase the area that must be repainted. Keep in mind that painting all the way up to the edge of a panel will require an absolutely perfect color match. The objective is to avoid this by allowing yourself a large blending area to compensate for any minor differences between the new paint and the existing finish. For a small dent in a quarter panel, you would perform the dent repair followed by the primer coats and block sanding,

again making sure to keep your work area to a minimum. When the area is ready to begin painting, you can then apply the color until full coverage is achieved, then you can gradually blend the paint application away from the repair and into the existing paint. Once the color is successfully applied, you can add the clearcoat if necessary, followed by a blending solvent to cut the dry spray at the blend. Once it's cured, you can buff and glaze as normal.

Buffing and Detailing

Customers will sometimes hear a shop tell them: "It will rub out, so bring it back in two weeks and we will rub it out." Quite often, that's just a way to appease an unhappy customer and get him out of the shop.

What will buff out is a slight run in the paint and most orange peel if the paint is not a heavy metallic finish, such as silver. Many metallics actually have small pieces of aluminum dust suspended in the paint to give it that sparkle. Since aluminum oxidizes when exposed to the oxygen in the air for any extended period of time, buffed silver will start to dull very quickly unless you top coat it again with a clear to protect it. Buffing a car will eliminate most small imperfections on the surface. Buffing is normally preceded by a color sanding of the paint with a soft rubber block to flatten the surface as much as possible. This is the scary part, especially if you did not paint he car and have no idea how thick the paint is. Many times the block sanding will cut through an edge or even a flat

Brian gets one last close-up look at the paint before breaking out the buffer.

Just as in sanding, finer and finer buffing compounds bring out the shine in a finish. We start with Meguiar's 84, which is the compound power cleaner, then go to 83, which is the dual action cleaner/polish and end with the 82, which is the swirl-free polish. We then jump ship to a 3M swirl removing compound that we have been using for years.

Paint Basics

After rough buffing the front fender, Brian takes a long look at the car to see how things are progressing. Looking down the length of the car, not straight at a fender, will reveal even the smallest imperfection.

Pneumatic polishers from Chicago Pneumatic or Ingersoll Rand work well with shop-supplied air. Milwaukee makes a nice electric buffer for shops that do not have a good air supply available or if you just like electric better than air. They both have advantages and disadvantages.

To begin buffing, simply apply the compound from the bottle onto the area of the car that you want to buff out.

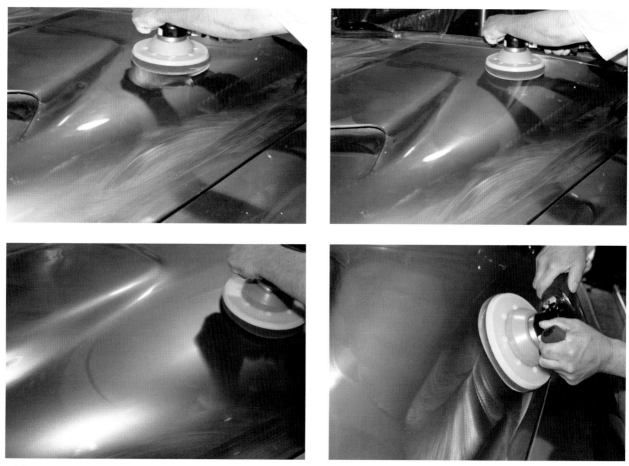

Without the buffer turned on, use the pad to swirl the compound around on the surface. Remember to always keep the buffer moving or you will burn the paint.

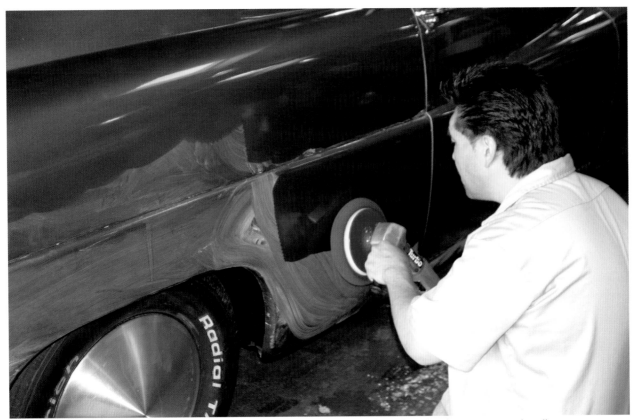

We have just started using the foam pads in our shop. It's a little early for me to endorse them, but they seem to work well.

surface and turn what would otherwise be a simple buffing into a major repaint.

My worst customer was a guy who had this horrible silver Buick that he loved — I believe he was the original owner. The car had a smashed-up front fender that his insurance company was going to cover the cost on, well part of it anyway — after his $500 deductible. He informed me that he lived right down the block from me and was a "neighbor" and on a fixed income, so I agreed to cover his deductible bringing the repair down to $500 from $1,000. It turned out his car was faded and pealing from one end to the other; living near the beach did not help either probably. But I agreed to give him a very considerable discount on a complete paint job if we did it at the time of the repair. He agreed and we painted his car, breaking even but maintaining goodwill in the neighborhood. You have heard the saying "no good deed goes unpunished." Well the car came out perfect … except for one very small speck (fly dropping) in the center of his trunk. It was so small he had trouble pointing it out to me. I explained to him that silver is a very hard color to touch up and I did not want to buff it out as we could break through the clear, (he did not want to pay additional for an extra coat of clear so we "gave" him a light coat just to add more gloss.) He was insistent that we fix our "screw up" and there was no reasoning with him, so I tried to buff out the trunk. Of course, we hit the silver during buffing, could not get the area to match the surrounding area, tried to touch up the paint in that area, one thing led to another, and we wound up repainting the

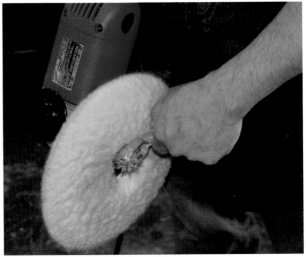

Yes, there is a tool for cleaning your buffing pad as it loads up with compound during buffing. Try to do this about every five minutes to keep from burning the paint.

trunk and trying to blend the paint down the side. After painting the car three times he was still not happy, and then he wanted the car stripped to the metal and repainted again. It was at the point that I said no, he took me to court and won all his money back. If the judge had seen the car before we started he would have thought we pulled off a miracle, but looking at 8 x 10 glossy photos of a dust speck magnified 3000 times made us look bad. Believe it or not, when everything was said and done, the guy had the gall to come by my shop and ask me to paint his car "red" this time. I said no. On occasion I still see his silver car and it

Film Thickness Defined

Paint is measured in mils, and an average paint job from the factory is 3.5 to 8 mils thick, depending on when the car was painted and the type of paint that was used. A mil is 1/1000 inch. The average piece of paper is about 3.5 mils thick, so you do not have lot to play with. If you then divide the thickness of a paint job into layers of primer, paint and clear you can see that a few mills is the most you are going to have to for protection over your base coat color. This is 1/3 the thickness of a single sheet of paper.

Very small high spots can sometimes be buffed out, but this is assuming that the paint is a solid non-metallic color, or the metallic has a lot of clear on it.

Above are three different types of film thickness gauges. The Positest DFT (left) offers digital accuracy with a readout in either mils or microns. The Positest DFT is available in the Ferrous model, which is used on steel-bodied vehicles, or the DFT Combo model, which can measure coatings on non-magnetic surfaces such as aluminum, brass or stainless. The Pro Motorcar Products ETG gauge is also digital, but requires contacting the painted surface with a tiny pinpoint stylus and applying a slight pressure. The most common and least expensive is the pen-style gauge such as the Pro Gauge II pictured here. After using all three types of gauges, I noted some obvious drawbacks with the pen style in terms of readability, accuracy and repeatability. But, with the Pro Gauge II price in the $50 range and the digitals costing a couple hundred dollars or more, some compromises were expected.

still looks good after 30-plus years. I guess it did rub out.

How do you buff out a mistake? Well, buffing starts with ultra-fine color sanding. By fine I mean really fine 3,000-grit. This is used to smooth out all the minor irregularities remaining on the surface of a car. What sanding or buffing cannot help are significant mistakes in the bodywork or a paint finish that is too thin.

Heavy metallic paint without a clearcoat is bad news, and buffing it will only give you a shine for a few weeks as the aluminum gets attacked by the oxygen on the air and starts to oxidize. The only cure for this, assuming the paint is good, is to lay a coat of clear over the paint job to help save it once it has been buffed out or sanded with a fine grit paper. Not many shops or painters would ever spray a heavy metallic without a clear coat anyway, so when problem happens it is more often a case of a decent good paint job being been buffed out too many times removing the top coat or clear. Each time you buff a car out you remove 1/1000 of an inch or so of clear or paint, and since the average paint job is about 8/1000 of an inch, it doesn't take long to get down through the clear, or even through the paint itself.

Chapter Ten

Common Paint Problems and Cures

There is no such thing as a perfect paint job. To qualify that statement, let me say that there is no perfect paint job straight out of the booth. This chapter deals with the dreaded problems that all painters both good and bad will eventually encounter. Even factory-applied paint jobs have a small amount of orange peel texture, so don't feel bad if your first attempt at spraying turns out a little rough. Paint problems, flaws, blemishes, imperfections, whatever you choose to call them, are unavoidable. Part of learning how to paint is learning how to handle problems.

Like any form of troubleshooting, the first step is to be able to identify the problem. Only then will you be able to determine the best solution. Unfortunately, identifying unusual reactions of the chemical kind is not an easy task, especially during the process of the actual paint job. What I've attempted to do for you here is to simulate some common paint problems through the magic of Photoshop, and then prescribe the best and most effective way to avoid them in the future or deal with them when they happen.

In learning how to become proficient at applying automotive paint you will also learn how to become an expert at solving paint-related problems. I think most shop owners and managers who rely on their painters will agree when I say that a good painter is not necessarily someone who can lay down a smooth coat of paint. A good painter is someone who can quickly handle paint problems as they occur and prevent the even more dreaded redo.

We learn by our mistakes and by our effort to repair those mistakes. Mistakes are good for training but bad for business. I have made my share of mistakes and have learned from most of them.

Just about the time you learn your equipment and the chemistry of the product you are using, it will change. A new system will come along or the paint manufacturer will change their formula for reasons that only they know. I have been through the nitrocellulose lacquer, acrylic lacquer, water-based paint, pressure pots, siphon feed guns and high-pressure guns. Now that is all gone and how long until the current product and equipment is obsolete?

Most paint problems are based on the materials as well as the equipment, or a combination of both of them, and are very hard to diagnose. For instance, using the mathematical law of compound probability and if there are five possibilities of mechanical reasons for a problem, and five chemical reasons for the same problem, the answer could be one of 25 (5x5) different things that could cause the problem. When you take into account the many different variables that are involved in the single burst of spray emitting from your gun's nozzle, it is amazing that anyone gets a good paint job. Many of the variables are common-sense solutions so we just "know" what to do, but some are not all that simple and we need constant communications with the gun or paint manufacturers to keep us up to date.

The best way to keep on top of paint problems is to study them when they occur. Don't just cover them up with more paint and hope they will not pop up in the future, try to analyze each and every one of them and find out what caused the problem and how to prevent it if it should ever happen again. Visit painters' Web sites (of which there

are many, just search under automotive paint problems) and see if anyone had the same problem. The Sharpe Mfg. Web site has an excellent Q&A section that covers many paint-related questions. Go so far as making notes and keeping a log of the problem as well as what worked to solve it. This will help you in the future or someone else if this information is shared with others. As an example I found this Web site that shows lots of answers to the paint problems we have listed; *(http://www.members.tripod.com/ ~bobstory/faq.html#Adjusting%20Paint%20Gun0).*

I have gotten to the point that I almost like finding a paint problem, just to try and figure out the cause as well as the solution to the problem. It's a challenge, and I love a challenge. I just don't like problems when we are on a deadline. The feeling of knowing how to fix something is one of the best feelings you can have.

There is no simple or single resolution to paint problems. For example, consider the simple "run in the paint." It is rare that a painter does not get a run somewhere in a paint job. A run could be caused by any number of things. Using too much air pressure can produce runs, or just holding the gun too close to the body of the car will, in effect, produce a higher pressure. Moving a gun too slowly will also cause a run.

Properly mixed paint can easily run if the gun technique is not correct. Then throw in the fact that a bit too much thinner or the wrong thinner can also make the paint run, as can the wrong ratio or not adding catalyst to a catalyzed paint. Take the above reasons and mix them together, so you now have the wrong ratio of paint to reducer in combination with too high of an air pressure setting and you have a whole new cause for a run or combinations of caused for a run.

If someone says "I have a run in my paint, what do you think caused it?" you cannot answer without having more information. This holds true for most paint problems.

I have seen paint problems that I have never figured out. I repaired them without knowing why they happened in the first place, they never came back and to this day it still bothers me. You will stumble on problems that require a repaint, and not know how to fix them. Hopefully these will be few a far between.

On another subject, I have noticed, and I don't know why, but when we have to turn out a perfect paint job, we have nothing but paint problems. On the other hand, when we have to do a movie car, which is not that critical (as most movie cars are internally dulled down to eliminate camera reflection), the jobs comes out flawless. The only thing I can attribute to this conundrum is that we are much more relaxed on the movie car than we are on the car that has to come out perfect. So, even stress has an effect on the outcome of a paint job.

I am not recommending having a good stiff drink before you enter the booth, but try to relax and assume that the job will come out without a problem. Chances are, it will. If not, then is the time for that drink.

Bleach (sometimes miss-referred to as Blushing or Bleeding)

Appearance: A general fading of a color, mostly involving older candy or pearl paint jobs.

Cause: No UV protection in the paint or the use of older paints. Some of the old pearls used fish scales or ground-up abalone shells that faded with exposure to sunlight.

Prevention: Use newer materials with UV protection in them. Follow paint manufacturer's recommendation for reduction.

Repair: A full repaint.

Blister

Appearance: A small convex or dome-like "blister" or bubble in the paint.

Cause: Trapped gas escaping through sub layers of the paint or in the bodywork fillers.

Prevention: Make sure that all air pockets or areas that can trap gas, such as pinholes, are removed.

Repair: In a small area the repair can be as simple as spot painting. If the problem is widespread, the whole car may need to be repainted after the air pockets in the bodywork are eliminated.

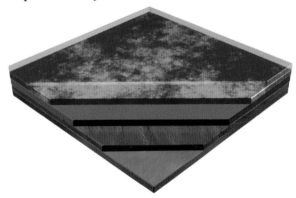

Blush

Appearance: A milky white haze. You will see it more on black and darker colors, but all paints can blush.

Cause: It is caused by moisture in the color or clearcoat. The moisture gets into the paint when the paint is sprayed in an environment that is too humid. Spraying during a rain shower, during the cooler part of a moist day and spraying a very heavy coat on a warm, humid day increases the chances of blushing.

Prevention: Use of the proper reducer is critical if humidity or rain is in the air. Heat lamps can also be a blessing.

Repair: Stop as soon as you see blushing or you will bury it under the paint and never be able to repair it. Sometimes, you can sand our buff out the area and continue the paint job on a warmer, drier day.

Bleed

Appearance: An unwanted color showing as small or large splotches on the finish.

Cause: Color from a previous paint job is coming through to the new top coat. Normally, this is a darker color or a red (bleeding) upward. Some plastic filler catalysts will also bleed through a paint job, as will permanent marker pens.

Prevention: You can use a bleeder sealer, but this doesn't guarantee that the bleed-through will stop. Your best bet is to avoid painting over anything that can possibly bleed. This includes red-catalyzed plastic filler, old finishes (esp. red), and marker pen ink. Always use a surface cleaning solvent before sanding.

Repair: Repainting is required. You may want to sand away the bleeding material, or you can try sanding and recoating with a barrier such as a water-borne primer.

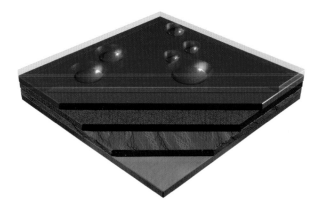

Cratering

Appearance: Deep pits in the paint.

Cause: A number of things can result in cratering. One of them is a poor attempt to bury a fisheye with more paint. If you lay more paint over a problem it only gets more pronounced. A small pit can become a large crater as you add more paint on top of it.

Repair: If it is not from a fisheye, stop as soon as you see the problem developing and fix the problem. Don't paint over it until it is sanded and smooth.

Cracking

Appearance: A split or crack in the paint.

Repair: Sand the area so that you obtain proper adhesion, making sure that the base metal is not rusty or split. Repaint the area.

Dry Spray

Appearance: The finish looks like sandpaper.

Cause: Shooting the wrong ratio of paint to thinner or holding the gun too far away form the surface of the car when painting.

Prevention: Mix the paint with the correct reducer (temperature), or hold the gun closer to the car.

Repair: In many cases the paint can be buffed out to a shine.

Drip/run

Appearance: *A* drip or run in the paint.

Cause: Too much paint, or too thin of a coat.

Prevention: Shoot a drier spray (less thinner) or lighter coats, or wait longer between coats.

Repair: Most runs can be sanded out, unless you are shooting a metallic or pearl.

Dust

Appearance: *Small, lumpy surface on the paint.*
Cause: Unclean surface.
Prevention: Thoroughly blow and wipe the surface.
Repair: The dust should be sanded out and the area repainted.

Fading

Appearance: A dulling in the color.
Cause: Generally, long periods of sun exposure.
Repair: Buffing is a possible fix, but in most cases the area will need to be repainted.

Fisheye

Appearance: Small, circular separations in the paint somewhat resembling a fish's eye.

Cause: The most common cause is contamination on the surface of the car. Contamination can result from any number of things, from greasy hands to silicone tire dressing to improperly evacuated air conditioning systems.

Prevention: Use a good silicone wax remover prior to sanding and the two-rag system for removing the wax — one rag to put the remover on and the other rag to remove it. This will lessen the recontamination of the surface. If fisheyes appear during a paint job, stop and add an eliminator that is compatible with the paint you're using.

Repair: The area will have to be sanded down and prepped and re-shot with new paint.

Flaking

Appearance: Paint coming off the car in flakes.
Cause: Poor adhesion from rust or a dirty surface, or improperly prepared metal.
Prevention: Sand the surface down thoroughly and make sure there is no rust present.
Repair: Repaint the area.

Mottling

Appearance: A fresh coat of metallic paint that has an uneven appearance.

Cause: When a metallic paint is applied too heavy or if the reducer is too slow drying. In either case, the layer of fresh paint tends to move until it sets up, causing the toners and metallic particles to swirl and collect in certain spots.

Prevention: Use the correct temperature reducer, apply the paint as recommended by the manufacturer, and allow adequate flash time between coats.

Repair: Repaint the area.

Orange Peel

Appearance: A glossy but slightly textured surface. All paint jobs, even factory ones, will have a certain degree of peel, unless it is color-sanded and rubbed out.

Cause: In most cases it is from not mixing the paint properly (not enough reducer), or having the gun too far from the surface of the car when painting. Excessive air pressure in the gun is another possible cause.

Prevention: Reduce the air pressure in the gun, use the correct ratio of reducers or hold the gun closer to the paint.

Repair: Many times it can be sanded and buffed to a smooth, flat finish.

Overspray

Appearance: Dry rough surface near and adjacent panel that was just painted.

Cause: Not masking off the contiguous panels when painting.

Prevention: Better masking.

Repair: Can often be sanded and buffed to a smooth, flat finish.

Pinholes

Appearance: Small holes in the finish that appear to be made with a needle or a pin.

Cause: Inadequate preparation. Small air pockets in plastic filler that are not properly filled with glaze will reappear in the paint as pinholes.

Prevention: Prior to painting, closely inspect every square inch of the body. Look for tiny imperfections or holes in the primer or filler.

Repair: Repaint the area.

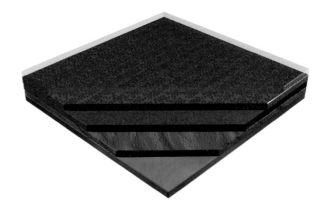

Polish/Swirl Marks

Appearance: Circular pattern of fine scratches in the paint.

Cause: Rotary polishers will leave swirl marks if the compound is too coarse or if the polisher speed is not correct.

Prevention: Use successively finer compounds and finish off with a non-abrasive swirl remover and a fine micro-fiber pad at the correct buffing speed.

Repair: Swirl marks can usually be removed simply by completing the buffing job with the proper compounds.

Solvent Pops

Appearance: Tiny, almost microscopic pinholes in fresh paint. Pops are not random, but rather uniformly spread out over the top surfaces.

Cause: Incorrect reducer speed.

Prevention: Use the correct temperature reducer for the spraying environment.

Repair: Repaint the area.

Rust

Appearance: Rust begins to surface as a bubbling in the paint. The bubbling patches continue to grow until the rust is treated.

Cause: Rust usually begins to form whenever damage occurs. Anything from a dent to a deep scratch can expose a bare metal surface for rust to begin.

Prevention: Treat the undercarriage and inner fender surfaces to an undercoating periodically. If the body is ever dented, check the backside of the damage after the repair is made. It may need another protective undercoating.

Repair: Complete metal repair and repaint of the area.

Scratch

Appearance: Line or gouge in the finish.

Prevention: Nothing, other than be careful and hope for good luck.

Repair: Sand and repaint the area.

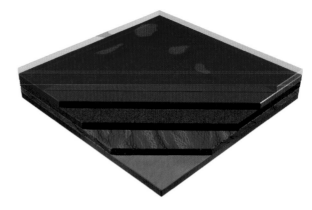

Tiger Stripes

Appearance: An uneven application of metallic particles, oftentimes in a randomly striped pattern.

Cause: A metallic paint applied by an inexperienced painter will reveal the back-and-forth spraying motion of the painter's gun.

Prevention: Most metallic paints must be evened out during the final coats to eliminate the uneven metallic pattern.

Repair: Repaint the area

Water Spots

Appearance: Depending on when they occur (during or after the vehicle is painted) they could be circular indentations in the paint or just discolorations in the paint. The shape is generally round.

Cause: Water getting into the paint during shooting from the roof of the booth, a hose hitting water on the ground or a painter dripping a bead of sweat. If it is water spots that have happened after the paint job, these are probably just discolorations from the calcium in the water and in most cases can be buffed or rubbed out.

Prevention: Keep the booth dry.

Repair: Repaint if the spots are in the bottom coat of paint, but if they are on the surface the spots can generally be buffed out.

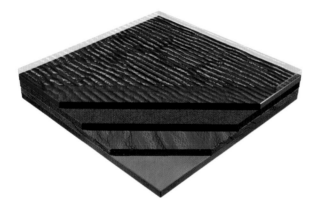

Lifting

Appearance: Lifting appears as a wrinkling in the fresh coat of paint.

Cause: Paint or primer will lift for several reasons. If the old finish was not properly catalyzed. If your flash time between coats is too long. If topcoats and undercoats are incompatible.

Repair: Repaint the area.

Chapter Eleven

Basic Paint and Body Dictionary

Words, Terms and Acronyms and What They Mean

A

ABRASIVE WHEEL: A grinding or cutting wheel composed of abrasive grits and a bonding agent to hold the grit together.

ACCELERATOR: Additive to paint to speed the cure of a coating. An additive to polyester resin that reacts with catalyst to speed up polymerization. This additive is required in room temperature cured resins. See promoter.

ACETONE: A solvent used to dissolve polyester resins. Used to a large extent for clean up of tools in fiberglass operations.

ACRYLIC: A plastic produced from acrylic acid or a derivative of. Material used in the manufacturing of paint to increase gloss and durability.

ADDITIVE: A chemical added to a paint to improve or create certain specific characteristics. Any number of materials used to modify the properties of polymer resins. Categories of additives include reagents, fillers, viscosity modifiers, pigments and others.

ADHESION PROMOTER: Material used over an O.E.M. or cured insoluble finish to increase the adhesion of the topcoat.

ADHESION: The state in which two surfaces are held together at an interface by forces or interlocking action or both.

AGING: The effect, on materials, of exposure to an environment for an interval of time; the process of exposing materials to an environment for an interval of time.

AIR DRY: The evaporation of solvent in an undercoat or topcoat at room temperature.

AK STEEL: Aluminum-killed steel treated with a strong deoxidizing agent, in this case, aluminum, to reduce oxygen content that prevents the forming of pin holes as the steel solidifies. AK steel has a fine-grain structure and is more stable at high temperatures than non-treated steel.

ALLOY: Metal composed of two or more elements to produce a desired quality in the metal.

ALLOY STEEL: carbon steel with one or more elements added to produce a desired quality.

ALUMINUM PIGMENT: Small aluminum particles used in paint to reflect light. These flakes vary in size and polish to give a look of glamour and luster.

ANNEAL: to heat metal to a specific temperature followed by controlled cooling to produce a desired quality. Usually to induce softness.

ANSI: American National Standards Institute

ARC WELDING: A welding process using heat produced by an electric arc.

ASPECT RATIO: The ratio of length to diameter of a fiber.

ASTM: American Society for Testing and Materials

ATOMIZE: The breaking-up of paint into fine particles or droplets by a paint gun.

B

BAKE: The process of applying heat to a finish to speed the cure or dry time of the finish.

BARE SUBSTRATE: Any material (steel, aluminum, plastic, etc.) that does not have a coating of paint or primer.

BASECOAT: A highly pigmented color that requires a coating of clear for protection, durability and gloss.

BASECOAT/CLEARCOAT SYSTEM: A two-stage finish consisting of a base color coat and a clear top coat.

BI-DIRECTIONAL: Reinforcing fibers that are arranged in two directions, usually at right angles to each other.

BINDER: A resin soluble adhesive that secures the random fibers in chopped strand mat or continuous strand roving.

BLEEDING: When soluble dyes or pigments in old finishes or filler are dissolved by solvents in topcoats, resulting in discoloration of the final finish.

BLENDING: Method of spray painting in which new finishes or colors overlap existing finishes or colors so slight differences cannot be distinguished. A gradual transition of one color into another as with multicolor flames.

BLISTERING: Effect of pressure from trapped solvent or moisture under a coating causing a swelling or blister in the finish; i.e. water blister. A flaw either between layers of laminate or between the gel coat film and laminate.

BLUSHING: A cloudy appearance of a topcoat that occurs when high humidity is present in the painting environment. When a fast-drying paint such as lacquer is applied, water condenses and becomes trapped in the wet coating. This can be eliminated by use of heat or a slower solvent or retarder.

BODY FILLER: A moldable catalyst-activated polyester-based plastic material used on bare substrate to fill dents in damaged auto body parts.

BOND STRENGTH: The amount of adhesion between bonded surfaces; a measure of the stress required to separate a layer of material from the base to which it is bonded.

BRAZE WELDING: a welding process in which the filler metal has a melting point below that of the base metal. Brass rod with a flux coating is most commonly used with steel.

BRIDGING: Occurrence where a primer or surfacer does not totally fill a sandscratch or imperfection. Not usually apparent in undercoat, however, does show up in topcoat.

BRITTLE: The quality of a paint coating that lacks flexibility.

BUBBLES: Air or solvent trapped in a paint film caused by poor atomization during spraying. Air trapped in body filler caused by excessive agitation.

BUFFING/COMPOUNDING: Using a mild abrasive compound or clay to bring out gloss and/or remove texture in a topcoat. This can be performed by hand or machine.

BURN/BURN THROUGH: Polishing or buffing of a color or clear too hard or long in one spot causing the underlying coat(s) to be revealed.

CAD: computer-aided design

CAM: computer-aided machining

CNC: computer numerical control

CASTING: The process of pouring a mixture of resin, fillers and/or fibers into a mold as opposed to building up layers through lamination. This technique produces different physical properties from laminating.

CATALYST: Technically considered an initiator, catalyst is the name given to the chemical added to resin or gel coat to initiate cure. Additive for paint to enhance the curing process.

CELLULOSE: Natural polymer or resin derived from cottonseed oil to make paint coatings.

CHALKING: The result of weathering of a paint film resulting in a white powdery appearance.

CHECKING: Sometimes called crow's feet. Tiny cracks or splitting in the surface of a paint film usually seen in a lacquer. Caused by improper film formation or excessive film build.

CHEMICAL STAIN/SPOTTING: Circular, oblong or irregular spots or discoloration on areas of finish caused by reactive chemicals coming into contact with air pollution (coal and high sulfur emissions), acid rain and snow.

CHIPPING: Removal of finish usually due to the impact of rocks and stones.

CHOP: Reducing the height of the top of a car by "Chopping" out a section of material from a horizontal section of the roof near the windows area.

CHOPPED STRAND MAT: A fiberglass reinforcement consisting of short strands of fiber arranged in a random pattern and held together with a binder.

COAT/SINGLE: Application of undercoat or topcoat over the surface using a 75% overlap of spray. Overlap recommendation varies between paint types, manufacturers, and painter's technique.

COAT/DOUBLE: Two single coats with longer flash time.

COLORANT: Made with ground pigments, solvent and resin. Used in the intermix system to produce colors.

COLOR COAT: The application of color to a prepared surface.

COLOR MATCH: Two separate applications of paint exhibiting no perceptible difference in color shade or tone when viewed under the same conditions.

COLOR RETENTION: The ability of a color to retain its true shade over an extended period of time. A color that is color fast.

COLOR STANDARD: A small sprayed-out sample of OEM color. This is the established requirement for a given color code. This is the color the car is supposed to be from the factory.

COMPLEMENTARY COLORS: Colors that are opposite each other on the color wheel.

COMPRESSIVE STRENGTH: The stress a given material can withstand when compressed. Described in ASTM D-695.

CONCENTRATION: The ratio of pigment in paint to resins in paint.

COVERAGE: The ability of a pigmented color to conceal or cover a surface.

CRATERING: The forming of holes in a film due to contamination.

CRAZING: Fine line cracks in the surface of the paint finish. Cracking of gel coat or resin due to stress.

CROSSCOAT: Applying paint in a crisscross pattern. Single coat applied in one direction with a second single coat applied at 90 degrees to the first.

CROW'S FEET: See Checking.

CURE: The chemical reaction of a coating during the drying process, leaving it insoluble.

CURDLING: The gelling or partial cure of paint due to incompatible materials.

CURTAINS: Large sagging or runs of paint due to improper application.

CUT IN: Painting of the edges of parts before installation.

CURE TIME: Time between introduction of catalyst or initiator to a polymer and final cure.

CURING AGENT: A catalytic or reactive agent which when added to a resin causes polymerization; synonymous with hardener.

CYCLE: The complete, repeating sequence of operations in a process or part of a process. In molding, the cycle time is the period (or elapsed time) between a certain point in one cycle and the same point in the next.

D

DEFINED ORIENTATION: The dispersion of metallic or mica flake with a definite pattern.

DELAMINATION: The peeling of a finish having improper adhesion. The separation of composite layers from each other.

DENSITY: A comparison of weight per volume, measured in pounds per cubic foot.

DEPTH: Lighter or darker in comparing two colors. The first adjustment in color matching.

DIE-BACK: The gradual loss of gloss due to continued evaporation of solvent after polishing.

DIMENSIONAL STABILITY: A description of the change in size of an object during the molding process or in varying temperature conditions or under various loads.

DIRECT (FACE): The color viewed from head-on (90°).

DISPERSION LACQUER: Particles of lacquer paint suspended or dispersed in a solvent that is not strong enough for total solution.

DISTORTION: A change in shape from that which is intended.

D.O.I. (DISTINCTNESS OF IMAGE): How clear a finish reflects an image.

DOUBLE COAT: One single coat of paint followed immediately by another.

DRAFT: The angle of the vertical components of a mold which allow removal of the part.

DRIER: A material used in a paint that enables it to cure.

DRY: The evaporation of solvent from a paint film.

DRY FILM THICKNESS (D.F.T.): The thickness of paint after it has dried and/or cured. Measured in mils.

DRY SPOT: Area of incomplete surface film on laminated plastics; in laminated glass, an area over which the interlayer and the glass have not become bonded.

DRY SPRAY: The process of applying paint in a lighter or not as wet application.

DURABILITY: How well a film weathers and lasts.

E

ELASTIC LIMIT: The greatest stress that a material is capable of sustaining without damage. A material is said to have passed its elastic limit when the load is sufficient to initiate plastic, or non-recoverable, deformation.

ELECTROSTATIC PAINT APPLICATION: Process of applying paint by having the surface electrically charged positive or negative and the application equipment on opposite electric charge.

ETCH: The process of chemically treating a material with an acid for corrosion resistance and adhesion of a primer, or to remove rust.

ETCHING PRIMER: A primer that contains an acid which etches the substrate as well as applying a primer. Protects against corrosion.

F

FACTORY PACKAGE COLOR (F.P.C.): Car colors that are matched, produced and packaged by paint manufacturers for specific car color codes for use in refinishing.

FADING: A gradual change of color or gloss in a finish.

FEATHEREDGE: A sanding process of tapering a broken paint edge to a smooth finish.

FEATHERING: Slang term for blending or slowly moving the edge of one color into a second color.

FEMALE MOLD: A concave mold used to precisely define the convex surface of a molded part.

FIBER ORIENTATION: Fiber alignment in a non-woven or a mat laminate where the majority of fibers are in the same direction, resulting in a higher strength in that direction.

FIBERGLASS: Glass that has been extruded into extremely fine filaments. These filaments vary in diameter, and are measured in microns. Glass filaments are treated with special binders and processed similar to textile fibers. These fibers come in many forms such as roving, woven roving, mat and continuous strands.

FIBERGLASS CLOTH: A fiberglass reinforcement made by weaving strands of glass fiber yarns. Cloth is available in various weights measured in ounces per square yard or kg/m2.

FILLER: Usually an inert organic or inorganic material that is added to plastic, resin or gel coat to vary the property, extend volume, or lower the cost of the article being produced.

FILM BUILD: The wet or dry thickness of applied coating measured in mils (also see DRY FILM THICKNESS).

FISH EYE: The effect of surface contamination that causes a circular separation of a paint or gel coat.

FLAKE-OFF: Large pieces of paint or undercoat falling off of substrate; also called delamination.

FLAMMABILITY: A measure of how fast a material will burn under controlled conditions.

FLASH/TIME: The time needed to allow solvents to evaporate from a freshly painted surface before applying another coat or heat.

FLATTENING AGENT: Material used in paint to dull or eliminate gloss.

FLEX AGENT: Material added to paint for additional flexibility, usually used for rubber or plastic flexible parts.

FLOATING: Characteristics or some pigments to separate from solution and migrate to the surface of paint film while still wet.

FLOP (SIDE TONE): The color of a finish when viewed from a side angle, other than direct.

FLUORESCENT LIGHT: Light emitted from a standard fluorescent fixture.

FLOW: The leveling properties of a wet paint film.

FOGCOAT: A final atomized coat of paint, usually applied at higher air pressure and at greater distance than normal to aid in distributing the metallic particles of paint into an even pattern.

FOAM: A lightweight, cellular plastic material containing gas-filled voids. Typical foams include urethane, PVC and polyester.

FOAM-IN-PLACE: The process of creating a foam by the combination of two liquid polymers.

FORCE DRY: Speed of dry due to application of heat.

G

GEL: The irreversible point at which a polymer changes from a liquid to a semi-solid. Sometimes called the "B" stage.

GEL COAT: A surface coat of a specialized polyester resin, either colored or clear, providing a cosmetic enhancement and weatherability to a fiberglass laminate.

GEL TIME: The length of time from catalyzation to gel or "B" stage.

GLAZE: A non-abrasive polishing compound used to gain gloss and shine.

GLOSS: Reflectance of light from a painted surface. Measured at different degrees by instruments known as gloss meters.

GOOD SIDE: The side of a molding in contact with a mold surface.

GREEN: Resin that has not completely cured and is still soft and rubbery.

GRAYNESS: The amount of black or white in a specific color.

GRINDING: Operation using a coarse abrasive, usually a spinning disc to remove material such as metal, paint, undercoat, rust, etc.

GROUND COAT: Highly pigmented coat of paint applied before a transparent color to speed hiding.

GUIDE COAT: A mist coat of a different color, usually primer, to aid in getting a panel sanded straight. A dry contrasting color applied to prime prior to sanding. This coat remains in the low areas and imperfections during the sanding process. When removed, imperfections are eliminated.

H

HAND LAMINATE: The process of manually building up layers of fiberglass and resin using hand rollers, brushes and spray equipment.

HANDSLICK: The time it takes for a wet paint film to become ready for another coat of paint.

HARDENER: A substance or mixture added to a plastic composition to promote or control the curing action.

HIGH BAKE: The baking of a paint above 180 degrees F.

HIGH SOLID: Paints and undercoats that have a higher percentage of pigment and resin (film formers).

HIGH STRENGTH/HIGH CONCENTRATED: The amount of pigment in the volume solid portion is in a higher amount, more pigment vs. resin.

HIGH VOLUME LOW PRESSURE (HVLP): Spray equipment that delivers material at a low pressure of no more than 10 psi (at the air cap), however, with greater volume of atomized material.

HOLD-OUT (COLOR): The ability of an undercoat to stop or greatly reduce the topcoat from soaking into it.

HUMIDITY: The amount or degree of water vapor, or moisture, in the air measured in percent.

HYGROSCOPIC: Capable of absorbing and retaining atmospheric moisture.

I

IMPACT STRENGTH: The ability of a material to withstand shock loading; the work done in fracturing a test specimen in a specified manner under shock loading.

IMPREGNATE: To saturate with resin. The most common application is saturating fiberglass with a catalyzed resin.

INCANDESCENT LIGHT: Light emitted from a burning filament in a glass bulb.

INCREMENT: A gradual increase in quantity.

INFRARED LIGHT: Portion of electromagnetic spectrum just below the visible light range. Can be used to cure paint due to heat being produced.

INNERCOAT ADHESION: The ability of one coat of paint to stick to another coat.

INSERT: A piece of material put into a laminate during or before molding to serve a definite purpose.

INTERMIX: The mixing of specific colors by adding different components or colorants to produce a usable mixture at the paint store or shop level.

ISOCYANATE/POLYISOCYANATE: toxic chemical material containing a functional group of nitrogen, carbon and oxygen, used in urethane catalyst and hardener to cross link material into a solid urethane film.

J

JOINT: A line or distinction formed when two panels are connected. Also referred to as a seam.

L

LACQUER: A type of paint that dries by solvent evaporation, which can be redissolved in its own solvent.

LAMINANT: The product of lamination. A composite consisting of a layer or layers of thermoset polymer and fiber reinforcement.

LAMINATE: To place into a mold a series of layers of polymer and reinforcement. The process of applying materials to a mold. To lay up.

LAMINATION: Applying a layer of glass and/or resin to a mold. Also used to describe a single ply of laminate.

LAY: In glass fiber, the spacing of the roving bands on the roving package expressed in the number of bands per inch; in filament winding, the orientation of the ribbon with some reference, usually the axis of rotation.

LAYER: A single ply of lay-up or laminate.

LAY-UP: The act of building up successive layers of polymer and reinforcement. Layers of catalyzed resin and fiberglass or other reinforcements are applied to a mold in order to make a part.

LET DOWN: The process of reducing the intensity of a colorant or mass tone through the addition of white or silver, allowing you to see cast and strength.

LIFTING: The soaking of a solvent into a soluble undercoat causing swelling, then causing the topcoat to wrinkle from underneath.

LOW-BAKE: Baking of a paint film up to 180 degrees F.

LOW PRESSURE COAT: The process of applying the final coat of paint at a lower air pressure. Used to uniform a finish or blending.

M

MALE MOLD: A convex mold where the concave surface of the part is precisely defined by the mold surface.

MASKING: Process of applying pressure, sensitive tape and paper to a vehicle to prevent paint from being applied where it is not wanted.

MASSTONE: The color of an undiluted colorant.

MASTER (PLUG): A full scale representation of the intended part, usually retained as a reference and the part from which production molds are made.

METHYL ETHYL KETONE: Solvent used in many paint reducers and thinners.

METALLIC COLOR: Colors containing various sizes of aluminum flakes. These flakes have reflective properties and when used in combinations and/or amounts, modify the optical characteristics of the color.

METAMERISM: A phenomenon exhibited by two colors that match under one or more light sources, but do not match under all light sources or viewing conditions.

MICA COLOR: Colors containing various sizes and/or colors of mica. Mica flakes have several optical characteristics allowing light to reflect, pass through and absorb. When added to color alone or with metallic flake, cause the color to look different depending on the angle of view.

MIG: metal inert gas welding

MIL: Relative to paint film thickness is a measurement equal to one-thousandth of an inch or .0254 millimeter. A typical factory-type paint consisting of an undercoat and topcoat should measure approximately 8 to 10 mils.

MINI BELL: Equipment used for electrostatic paint application consisting of a spinning disk to which paint is applied. The spinning disc is charged electrically and paint is atomized through centrifugal force.

MIST COAT: A thin sprayed coat to uniform metallic finishes. Also used to blend colors. Sometimes used with light amounts of solvents to uniform finish and/or increase gloss.

MOTTLING: Blotches of metallic or mica particles in a paint film.

MICROBALLOONS: Microscopic bubbles of glass, ceramic or phenolic, used as a filler or to create syntactic foam or putty mixtures.

MICRON: One micron = .001 millimeter = .00003937 inch.

MOLD: The tool used to fabricate the desired part shape. Also used to describe the process of making a part in a mold.

MOLDING: The process of using a mold to form a part.

MOLD RELEASE: A wax or polymer compound that is applied to the mold surface which acts as a barrier between the mold and the part, thus preventing the part from bonding to the mold.

MOLD SHRINKAGE: The immediate shrinkage which a molded part undergoes when it is removed from a mold and cooled to room temperature; the difference in dimensions, expressed in inches per inch between a molding and the mold cavity in which it was molded (at normal temperature measurement); the incremental difference between the dimensions of the molding and the mold from which it was made, expressed as a percentage of the dimensions of the mold.

M.S.D.S. (MATERIAL SAFETY DATA SHEET): Contains information and specifications on a chemical or material. M.S.D.S. data on specific chemicals or materials can be obtained from their respective manufactuers.

N

NITROCELLULOSE: A type of lacquer paint. Also refered to as "straight" lacquer.

O

ORANGE PEEL: A gel coated or painted finish that is not smooth and is patterned similar to an orange's skin.

P

PARTING AGENT: See Mold Release

PARTING LINE: The location on a molded product between different segments of the mold used to produce the product.

PATTERN: The initial model for making fiberglass molds. See Plug.

PEENING: Working of metal by hammer blows or shot blasting to increase hardness.

PLASMA: A gas heated to a high temperature which becomes ionized, thereby able to penetrate through metal.

PLUG: An industry term for a pattern or model.

POT LIFE: The time during which the catalyzed resin remains liquid or "workable." See Gel Time.

PRIMER-SURFACER: A sandable undercoat formulated to fill minute surface imperfections in preparation for paint.

PUTTY: A thickened mixture of resin made by adding fillers, thixotrophs and reinforcing fibers.

R

RELEASE AGENT: A compound used to reduce surface tension or adhesion between a mold and a part.

RESIN: A liquid polymer which when catalyzed cures to a solid state.

RUST: an oxidized iron. Also iron or iron alloy that has chemically reacted with exposure to oxygen and water.

S

SEALER: Material applied before topcoat to increase color holdout and uniformity of color and adhesion.

SEAM: See Joint.

SECONDARY COLORS: Mixture of two primary colors to produce a second color. Example: red and yellow make orange.

SEEDY: Rough or gritty appearance of paint due to very small insoluble particles.

SHADE: A variation of color. Example 1: a green shade blue. Example 2: light blue versus dark blue.

SHRINKAGE: The relative change in dimension between the length measured on the mold when it is cold and the length on the molded object 24 hours after it has been taken out of the mold. Also the tightening or shrinking of paint film as solvent evaporates.

SIDETONE "FLOP": The color of a finish when viewed from a side angle.

SINGLE STAGE: A one-step paint procedure of applying color, protection and durability in one application. No clear is used.

SIPHON FEED GUN: Any paint gun which uses air flowing over an opening to create a vacuum to draw paint up through a tube to be atomized.

SLAG: residual metal byproduct of welding processes.

S.M.C.: Sheet-molded compound, usually a polyester-based, fiberglass-reinforced material such as panels of a Corvette body.

SOLIDS: The part of the paint, pigments and resin which do not evaporate.

SOLID COLOR: Colors that contain no metallic flakes in the pigment portion of paint. These colors have opaque pigmentation or properties in the paint film.

SOLUTION: A homogeneous mixture of two or more dissimilar substances.

SOLVENT CLEANER: Solvent-based cleaning material used to remove contamination from surfaces prior to refinishing.

SOLVENT POP: Blisters in the surface of a film caused by trapment of solvent.

SPLITTING: The breaking open of an undercoat or topcoat into long cracks resembling the look of a "dry river bottom."

SPOT REPAIR: The process of repairing only a portion of a panel or vehicle.

SPRAY PATTERN: Spray from the paint gun adjusted from a very small, almost round pattern to a wide, flat, somewhat oval shape.

STABILIZER: Special resin-containing solvent used in basecoat color to lower viscosity helping in metallic control and recoat times.

STRENGTH OF COLOR: The hiding ability of a pigmented toner or colorant.

T

TACK: Surface stickiness.

TACK COAT: Usually the first light coat of paint is allowed to set and become sticky before additional coats are applied.

TACK FREE: Time in the drying of a paint film where it is not sticky but not completely cured.

TACK RAG: A sticky cheese cloth used to remove dust before painting.

TEXTURE: The amount of orange peel or roughness in a dried paint film.

THERMAL COEFFICIENT OF EXPANSION: Measures dimensional change of a material when heated or cooled. Measured in inches per inch per degree.

THERMOSPLASTIC PAINT: Material which, with the addition of heat, becomes soft and pliable, returning to solid when cooled; i.e., lacquer.

THERMOSETTING PAINT: Type of paint that becomes hard when heated and thereafter is cured; i.e., enamels, urethanes.

THINNER: Solvent material used to reduce the viscosity of lacquers.

THREE-STAGE SYSTEM: A three-step paint procedure.

First, a highly pigmented color coat is applied to achieve hiding — referred to as the groundcoat. This groundcoat is then followed by the intermediate coat. The intermediate coat is applied using a transparent mica in a number of single coats until the desired effect is obtained. This finish requires a clearcoat for gloss protection and durability, which is applied last.

TIG: Tungsten inert gas

TINT: A pure toner used for the changing of another color.

TINTING: The act of changing one color by adding another.

TITANIUM DIOXIDE: A commonly used white pigment with high hiding power.

TONERS: Made with ground pigments, solvent and resin. Used in the intermix system to produce colors.

TOPCOAT: The pigmented color portion of the painting process.

TOUGHNESS: The ability of a finish to withstand abrasion, scratches, etc.

TRANSFER-EFFICIENCY: The ratio in a percentage of the amount of paint actually applied to a surface compared to the amount of material used.

TRANSLUCENT: Permits a percentage of light to pass but not optically clear like window glass.

TWO-COMPONENT: A paint material which must have a catalyst or hardener to react.

U

ULTRA VIOLET (UV) LIGHT: The part of the electromagnetic spectrum that can cause fading of paint. Located just beyond the visible part of spectrum.

UNDERCOAT: The coatings below the top color coat that help in adhesion and corrosion resistance.

V

VISCOSITY: Measure of a fluid's quality of flow. Determined by allowing a measured amount to flow through an orifice and measuring the time it takes for this amount to flow.

V.O.C. (VOLATILE ORGANIC COMPOUND): Any organic compound that evaporates and subsequently participates in atmospheric photo-chemical reaction; that is, any organic compound other than those that the administrator designates as having negligible photochemical activity.

VISCOSITY: The liquid properties of a material. Resistance to flow.

VISCOSITY CUP: A tool used to meter the viscosity of paint to insure precise reduction.

W

WATERBORNE COATING: A coating containing more than five percent water in its volatile fraction.

WAX: A compound used as a release agent. See Release Agent.

Chapter Twelve

Manufacturer Source Guide

3M Company (abrasives, paint prep and metal treatment)
Web site: www.3M.com

Ajax Tool Works (air chisels, hand and power tool accessories)
10801 Franklin Avenue
Franklin Park, IL 60131
Phone: 800-323-9129
Web site: www.ajaxtools.com

Auto Body Toolmart (auto body and paint supplies, tools)
Phone: 800-382-1200
Web Site: www.autobodytoolmart.com

Back-a-line, Inc. (knee pads, back support belts)
644 111th Avenue
San Francisco, CA 94118
Phone: 800-905-2225
Web site: www.backaline.com

Bend-Pak (automobile lifts)
1645 Lemonwood Drive
Santa Paula, CA USA 93060
Local phone: 805-933-9970, toll-free phone: 800-253-2363
Web site: www.bendpak.com

Bessey Tools North America (clamps, snips, hammers)
1165 Franklin Blvd., Unit G / P.O. Box 490
Cambridge, ON N1R 5V5
Phone: 519-621-7240
Web site: www.americanclamping.com

Bosch Tools And Accessories (cordless and electric power tools)
Phone: 877-BOSCH-99
Web site: www.boschtools.com

Channellock, Inc. (pliers, cutters)
1306 South Main Street
Meadville, PA 16335
Phone: 800-724-3018
Web site: www.channellock.com

Chicago Pneumatic (pneumatic power tools)
Web site: www.chicagopneumatic.com

Craftsman (power and hand tools, tool storage, air compressors)
Web site: www.sears.com

Customs By Eddie Paul (design, custom cars, motorcycles, film/television vehicles, paint and fabrication work, CNC machining, video production)
2305 Utah Avenue
El Segundo, California 90245
Phone: 310-643-8515

Devilbiss Automotive Refinishing (painting equipment, spray guns, air regulators and filters)
Phone: 800-445-3988
Web site: www.autorefinishdevilbiss.com

Eagle Bending Machines (hydraulic tubing roller)
Phone: 251-937-0947
Web site: www.eaglebendingmachines.com

Eastwood Tools (restoration, autobody, paint and metal-working tools)
263 Shoemaker Road
Pottstown, PA 19464
Phone: 800-345-1178
Web site: www.eastwood.com

E. P. Industries, Inc. (metal fabrication tools, how-to videos/DVDs)
2305 Utah Avenue
El Segundo, CA 90245
Phone: 310-245-8515
Web site: www.epindustries.com

ESAB (welding equipment and consumables)
Web site: www.esab.com

Evercoat (body fillers, primers, metal treatment, fiberglass materials)
6600 Cornell Road
Cincinnati, OH 45242
Phone: 513-489-7600
Web site: www.evercoat.com

House of Kolor (custom automotive paint)
210 Crosby Street
Picayune, Mississippi 39466
Phone: 601-798-4229
Web site: www.houseofkolor.com

Hutchins Manufacturing Company (pneumatic sanders and accessories)
49 North Lotus Avenue
Pasadena, CA 91107
Phone: 626-792-8211
Web site: www.hutchinsmfg.com

Ingersoll Rand (pneumatic power tools)
Web site: www.irtools.com

Innova—Emissive Energy Corp. (L.E.D. flashlights)
135 Circuit Drive
N. Kingstown, RI 02852
Phone: 401-294-2030
Web site: www.innova.com

Irwin Industrial Tools (Vise Grips)
Web site: www.irwin.com

Lincoln Electric Company (welding equipment)
22801 St. Clair Avenue
Cleveland, OH 44117
Phone: 216-481-8100
Web site: www.lincolnelectric.com

Meguiar's Inc. (car care products, buffing and polishing compounds)
17991 Mitchell South
Irvine, CA 92614
Phone: 800-347-5700
Web site: www.meguiars.com

Milwaukee Electric Tool Corp. (cordless and electric power tools)
13135 W. Lisbon Road
Brookfield, WI 53005
Toll-free phone: 800-729-3878
Web site: www.milwaukeetool.com

Morgan Manufacturing, Inc. (Morgan "Nokker" slide hammers, accessories)
521 2nd Street
Petaluma, CA 94952
Phone: 800-423-4692
Web site: www.morganmfg.com

Motor Guard Corporation (Magna Spot welders)
580 Carnegie Street
Manteca, CA 95337
Phone: 209-239-9191
Web site: www.motorguard.com

National Detroit, Inc. (pneumatic sanding, grinding and buffing tools)
P.O. Box 2285
Rockford, IL 61131
Phone: 815-877-4041
Web site: www.nationaldetroit.com

P.B.E. Specialties (paint and body equipment)
13801 Kolter Road
Spencerville, OH 45887
Phone: 888-997-7416

Plasmacam, Inc. (CNC plasma-cutting machines)
P.O. Box 19818
Colorado City, CO 81019
Phone: 719-676-2700
Web site: www.plasmacam.com

POR-15, Inc. (rust preventative coatings and chemicals)
P.O. 1235
Morristown, NJ 07962
Phone: 800-726-0459
Web site: www.por15.com

PPG Industries (factory and custom automotive paint)
Web site: www.ppgrefinish.com

Ranger Products (floor jacks, stands, and tool storage)
1645 Lemonwood Drive
Santa Paula, CA USA 93060
Local phone: 805-933-9970, toll-free phone: 800-253-2363
Web site: www.rangerproducts.com

Ringers Gloves (work gloves, shoes)
335 Science Drive
Moorpark, CA 93021
Phone: 800-421-8454
Web site: www.ringersgloves.com

Sata (automotive painting equipment)
Web site: www.sata.com/usa/

Scotchman Industries (metal fabrication equipment)
180 E. Hwy 14
P.O. Box 850
Philip, SD 57567
Phone: 800-843-8844
Web site: www.scotchman.com

Sem Products, Inc. (custom paint, prep and repair products)
651 Michael Wylie Drive
Charlotte, NC 28217
Phone: 1-800-831-1122
Web site: www.sem.ws

Sharpe Manufacturing Company (spray guns and accessories)
P.O. Box 1441
Minneapolis, MN 55440
Phone: 800-742-7731
Web site: www.sharpe1.com

Slide Sledge (sliding hammer)
2500 W. Higgins Road
Hoffman Estates, IL 60195
Phone: 800-276-0311
Web site: www.slidesledge.com

Snap-On Tools (automotive tools and tool storage)
Web site: www.snapon.com

Tools USA—Standard Tools and Equipment (automotive spray booths, automotive tools)
4810 Clover Road
Greensboro, NC 27405
Toll-free phone: 800-451-2425
Web site: www.toolsusa.com

Tru-Line Laser Alignment
8231 Blaine Road
Blaine, WA 98230
Phone: 800-496-3777
Web site: www.tru-line.net

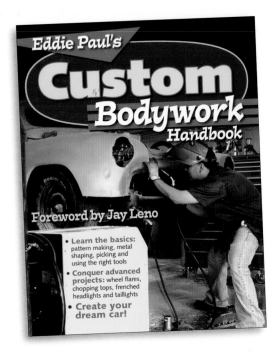
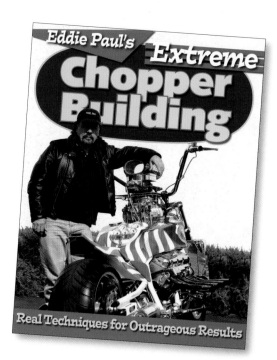